First World War
and Army of Occupation
War Diary
France, Belgium and Germany

42 DIVISION
Divisional Troops
Machine Gun Corps
42 Battalion
13 January 1918 - 30 June 1919

WO95/2650/5

The Naval & Military Press Ltd
www.nmarchive.com
Published in association with The National Archives

Published by

The Naval & Military Press Ltd

Unit 10 Ridgewood Industrial Park,

Uckfield, East Sussex,

TN22 5QE England

Tel: +44 (0) 1825 749494

www.naval-military-press.com

www.nmarchive.com

This diary has been reprinted in facsimile from the original. Any imperfections are inevitably reproduced and the quality may fall short of modern type and cartographic standards.

© Crown Copyright
Images reproduced by permission of The National Archives, London, England, 2015.

Contents

Document type	Place/Title	Date From	Date To
Heading	WO95/2650/5		
Heading	42 Bn Machine Gun Corps Jan 1918-Jun 1919		
Heading	War Diary 268th M.G. Coy Vol 1 Pages 1-3 Jan 1918		
War Diary	Grantham	13/01/1918	13/01/1918
War Diary	Southampton	14/01/1918	14/01/1918
War Diary	Havre	15/01/1918	19/01/1918
War Diary	Bethune Locon	20/01/1918	24/01/1918
War Diary	Locon	25/01/1918	31/01/1918
Heading	War Diary 268th M.G. Coy Vol F1 Page 4-6 Feb 1st-Feb 28th 1918		
War Diary	Gorre	01/02/1918	11/02/1918
War Diary	La Beuvriere	12/02/1918	28/02/1918
Heading	42nd Battalion, Machine Gun Corps. March 1918		
Heading	Original War Diary Of 42nd Battalion Machine Gun Corps From 1-3-18 To 31-3-18 (Volume I)		
War Diary	Labeuvriere	01/03/1918	04/03/1918
War Diary	Fouquieres	05/03/1918	22/03/1918
War Diary	Adinfer Wood	23/03/1918	26/03/1918
War Diary	Fonquevillers	27/03/1918	27/03/1918
War Diary	St Amand	28/03/1918	31/03/1918
Miscellaneous	Appendices 1, 2, 3 & 4.		
Miscellaneous	Appendix I		
Miscellaneous	C Form. Messages And Signals.		
Map	Sheet 36 A S.E.		
Miscellaneous	Training. Appendix II		
Operation(al) Order(s)	42nd. Battalion, M.G.C. Order No. 4. Appendix III	29/03/1918	29/03/1918
Miscellaneous	Reference Operation Order No. 4. Appendix III	29/03/1918	29/03/1918
Operation(al) Order(s)	42nd. Battalion, M.G.C. Order No. 5. Appendix IV	30/03/1918	30/03/1918
Heading	42nd Battalion, Machine Gun Corps. April 1918		
Heading	Original War Diary Of 42nd Battalion Machine Gun Corps. From 1-4-18 To 30-4-18 (Volume II)		
War Diary	St Amand	01/04/1918	03/04/1918
War Diary	Henu	04/04/1918	07/04/1918
War Diary	Authie	08/04/1918	13/04/1918
War Diary	Couin	14/04/1918	30/04/1918
Miscellaneous	Appendices I, II, III, IV, V, VI & VII.		
Operation(al) Order(s)	42nd. Battalion. M.G.C. Order No. 7. App. I	31/03/1918	31/03/1918
Operation(al) Order(s)	42nd. Battalion, M.G.C. Order No. 8. App II	01/04/1918	01/04/1918
Operation(al) Order(s)	42nd. Battalion, M.G.C. Order No. 9. App III	07/04/1918	07/04/1918
Miscellaneous	Warning Order. App. IV	14/04/1918	14/04/1918
Operation(al) Order(s)	42nd. Battalion, M.G.C. Order No. 11. App IV	15/04/1918	15/04/1918
Operation(al) Order(s)	42nd. Battalion, M.G.C. Order No. 12. App V	24/04/1918	24/04/1918
Operation(al) Order(s)	42nd. Battalion, M.G.C. Order No. 12. App VI	22/04/1918	22/04/1918
Operation(al) Order(s)	42nd. Battalion, M.G.C. Order No. 14. App VII	29/04/1918	29/04/1918
Heading	Original War Diary Of 42nd Battalion Machine Gun Corps From 1-5-18 To 31-5-18. (Volume 3)		
War Diary	Couin	01/05/1918	07/05/1918
War Diary	Pas.	08/05/1918	31/05/1918
Operation(al) Order(s)	42nd. Battalion, M.G.C. Order No. 15. App I	03/05/1918	03/05/1918

Miscellaneous	O.C.A. Coy. 42nd. Divn. "A". B. Coy. 42nd Divn. "Q". C. Coy. C.M.G.O. D. Coy. Batt. Transport Offr.	07/05/1918	07/05/1918
Miscellaneous	Training Programme For Tuesday, May 14th, 1918. App III	13/05/1918	13/05/1918
Miscellaneous	Training Programme For May, 14th 1918. App III	13/05/1918	13/05/1918
Miscellaneous	42nd. Battalion, Machine Gun Corps. Training Programme For Wednesday, May 15th, 1918. App IV	14/05/1918	14/05/1918
Miscellaneous	42nd. Battalion, Machine Gun Corps. Training Programme For Thursday, May 16th, 1918. App V	15/05/1918	15/05/1918
Miscellaneous	42nd. Battalion, Machine Gun Corps. Training Programme For Friday, May 17th, 1918. App VI	16/05/1918	16/05/1918
Miscellaneous	42nd. Battalion, Machine Gun Corps. Training Programme For Saturday, May 18th. 1918. App VII	17/05/1918	17/05/1918
Miscellaneous	42nd. Battalion Machine Gun Corps. Training Programme For Monday, May 20th, 1918. App VIII	19/05/1918	19/05/1918
Miscellaneous	42nd. Battalion, Machine Gun Corps. Training Programme For Wednesday, May 22nd, 1918. App IX	20/05/1918	20/05/1918
Miscellaneous	42nd. Battalion, Machine Gun Corps. Training Programme For Thursday, May 23rd, 1918. App X	21/05/1918	21/05/1918
Miscellaneous	42nd. Battalion, Machine Gun Corps. Training Programme For Friday, May 24th, 1918. App XI	22/05/1918	22/05/1918
Miscellaneous	42nd. Battalion, Machine Gun Corps. Training Programme For Saturday, May 25th, 1918. App XII	23/05/1918	23/05/1918
Miscellaneous	42nd. Battalion, Machine Gun Corps. Training Programme For Monday, May 27th, 1918. App XIII	25/05/1918	25/05/1918
Miscellaneous	42nd. Battalion, Machine Gun Corps. Training Programme For Wednesday, May 29th. 1918. App XV	27/05/1918	27/05/1918
Miscellaneous	42nd. Battalion, Machine Gun Corps. Training Programme For Tuesday, May 28th, 1918. App XIV	26/05/1918	26/05/1918
Miscellaneous	42nd. Battalion, Machine Gun Corps. Training Programme For Thursday, May 30th. 1918. App XVI	28/05/1918	28/05/1918
Miscellaneous	42nd. Battalion, Machine Gun Corps. Training Programme For Friday, May 31st, 1918. App XVII	29/05/1918	29/05/1918
Heading	War Diary. Of 42nd. Battalion Machine Gun Corps. From 1.6.18 To 30.6.18 (Volume IV)		
War Diary	Pas	01/06/1918	06/06/1918
War Diary	Bus	07/06/1918	30/06/1918
Miscellaneous	42nd. Battalion, Machine Gun Corps. Training Programme For Saturday, June 1st. 1918. App I	30/05/1918	30/05/1918
Miscellaneous	42nd. Battalion, Machine Gun Corps. Training Programme For Monday, June 3rd. 1918. App II	01/06/1918	01/06/1918
Miscellaneous	42nd. Battalion, Machine Gun Corps. Training Programme For Tuesday, June 4th. 1918. App III	02/06/1918	02/06/1918
Operation(al) Order(s)	42nd. Battalion, M.G.C. Order No. 16. App IV	02/06/1918	02/06/1918
Miscellaneous	42nd. Battalion, Machine Gun Corps. Training Programme For Wednesday, June 5th. 1918. App V	03/06/1918	03/06/1918
Operation(al) Order(s)	42nd. Battalion, M.G.C. Order No. 18. App VI	12/06/1918	12/06/1918
Operation(al) Order(s)	42nd. Battalion, M.G.C. Order No. 19. App. VI	23/06/1918	23/06/1918
Operation(al) Order(s)	42nd. Battalion, M.G.C. Order No. 20. App VIII	29/06/1918	29/06/1918
Heading	Original War Diary Of 42nd Battalion Machine Gun Corps. From 1-7-18 To 31-7-18		
War Diary	Bus	01/07/1918	09/07/1918
War Diary	I.23 Central	10/07/1918	15/07/1918
War Diary	Authie	16/07/1918	17/07/1918
War Diary	Bus	18/07/1918	31/07/1918
Operation(al) Order(s)	42nd. Battalion, M.G.C. Order No. 21.	08/07/1918	08/07/1918

Operation(al) Order(s)	42nd. Battalion, M.G.C. Order No. 22. App II	19/07/1918	19/07/1918
Heading	Original War Diary of 42nd. Battalion Machine Gun Corps. (Volume VI) From 1.8.18 To 31.8.18		
War Diary	Bus	01/08/1918	23/08/1918
War Diary	K.25 a. 0.4.	24/08/1918	26/08/1918
War Diary	L10.b. 5.6.	27/08/1918	29/08/1918
War Diary	G.29.d.9.6	30/08/1918	31/08/1918
Operation(al) Order(s)	42nd. Battalion, M.G.C. Order No. 23. App I	31/07/1918	31/07/1918
Operation(al) Order(s)	42nd. Battalion, M.G.C. Order No. 25. App II	12/08/1918	12/08/1918
Operation(al) Order(s)	42nd. Battalion, M.G.C. Order No. 26. App III	20/08/1918	20/08/1918
Heading	(Original) War Diary of 42nd. Battalion Machine Gun Corps From 1-9-18 To 30-9-18 Volume VII.		
War Diary	G29.d.9.6	01/09/1918	03/09/1918
War Diary	N5c.50.05	04/09/1918	04/09/1918
War Diary	N5c 5.1.	05/09/1918	05/09/1918
War Diary	M6 d. 3.5	06/09/1918	20/09/1918
War Diary	J 31 C. 4.7.	21/09/1918	21/09/1918
War Diary	I.29 d. 4.3	22/09/1918	22/09/1918
War Diary	I.36.d. 8.1.	23/09/1918	30/09/1918
Miscellaneous	Training Programme. For 10th. September 1918. App I	09/09/1918	09/09/1918
Operation(al) Order(s)	42nd. Battalion, M.G.C. Order No. 27. App II	18/09/1918	18/09/1918
Miscellaneous	App III		
Miscellaneous	Amendment To 42nd. Battalion, M.G.C. Order No. 27.	20/09/1918	20/09/1918
Miscellaneous	March Table to Accompany 42nd. Battn. M.G.C. Order No. 27.		
Miscellaneous	42nd. Battalion, M.G.C. Training Programme For Thursday, October 31st. 1918. App V	30/10/1918	30/10/1918
Map	App III		
Heading	(Original) War Diary of 42nd. Battalion Machine Gun Corps From 1-10-18 To 31-10-18 Volume VIII		
War Diary	I.36.d.8.1.	01/10/1918	06/10/1918
War Diary	Beauvois	01/10/1918	04/10/1918
War Diary	Le Quesnoy	05/10/1918	05/10/1918
War Diary	I.36.d.8.1.	06/10/1918	07/10/1918
War Diary	Q.10.C.1.1.	08/10/1918	08/10/1918
War Diary	Esnes	09/10/1918	11/10/1918
War Diary	Beauvois	12/10/1918	31/10/1918
Miscellaneous	42nd. Battalion, M.G.C. Training Programme for Thursday, October 3rd. 1918. App I	02/09/1918	02/09/1918
Operation(al) Order(s)	42nd. Battalion, M.G.C. Order No. 28. App II	08/10/1918	08/10/1918
Miscellaneous	O.C. A. Company. B. Company. C. Company. D. Company. 42nd. Division 'G' App II	06/05/1918	06/05/1918
Map	App. III		
Map	42nd. Battalion, M.G. Corps. Training Programme For Wednesday, October. 30th. 1918. App IV	29/10/1918	29/10/1918
Heading	(Original) War Diary Of 42nd Battalion Machine Gun Corps From 1-11-18 To 30-11-18 Volume IX		
War Diary	Le Quesnoy	05/11/1918	05/11/1918
War Diary	M.36.d. 1.7.	06/11/1918	07/11/1918
War Diary	Hargnies	08/11/1918	09/11/1918
War Diary	Hautmont	10/11/1918	30/11/1918
Heading	(Original) War Diary of 42nd Battalion M.G. Corps. From 1-12-18 To 31-12-18 Volume X		
War Diary	Hautmont	01/12/1918	13/12/1918
War Diary	Rocq	14/12/1918	14/12/1918
War Diary	Bonne Esperance	15/12/1918	15/12/1918

War Diary	Leernes	16/12/1918	17/12/1918
War Diary	Marchienne Au Pont	18/12/1918	18/12/1918
War Diary	Velaine	19/12/1918	31/12/1918
Miscellaneous	42nd. Battalion, M.G.C. Training Programme For Monday, December 2nd. 1918. App I	01/12/1918	01/12/1918
Miscellaneous	42nd. Battalion, M.G.C. Training Programme For Tuesday, December 3rd. 1918. App II	02/12/1918	02/12/1918
Miscellaneous	42nd. Battalion, M.G.C. Training Programme For Wednesday, December 4th. 1918. App III	03/12/1918	03/12/1918
Miscellaneous	42nd. Battalion, M.G.C. Training Programme For Thursday, December 5th. 1918. App IV	04/12/1918	04/12/1918
Miscellaneous	42nd. Battalion, M.G.C. Training Programme For Friday, December 6th. 1918. App V	05/12/1918	05/12/1918
Miscellaneous	42nd. Battalion, M.G.C. Training Programme For Saturday, December 7th. 1918. App VI	06/12/1918	06/12/1918
Miscellaneous	42nd. Battalion, M.G.C. Training Programme For Monday, December 9th. 1918. App VII	08/12/1918	08/12/1918
Miscellaneous	42nd. Battalion, M.G.C. Training Programme For Tuesday, December 10th. 1918. App VIII	09/12/1918	09/12/1918
Miscellaneous	42nd. Battalion, M.G.C. Training Programme For Wednesday, December 11th. 1918. App IX	10/12/1918	10/12/1918
Miscellaneous	42nd. Battalion, M.G.C. Training Programme For Thursday, December 12th. 1918. App X	11/12/1918	11/12/1918
Heading	(Original) War Diary of 42nd. Battalion M.G.C. From 1-1-19 To 31-1-19 Volume I		
War Diary	Velaine	01/01/1919	31/01/1919
Miscellaneous	Training Programme. 1st. January, 1918. App I		
Miscellaneous	42nd. Battalion M.G.C. Training Programme For Thursday 2nd. January 1918. App II	01/01/1919	01/01/1919
Miscellaneous	Training Programme for 3/1/19. 42nd. Battalion, M.G.C. App III	02/01/1919	02/01/1919
Miscellaneous	42nd Battalion, Machine Gun Corps. Training Programme For Saturday, January 4th 1919. App IV	03/01/1919	03/01/1919
Miscellaneous	42nd Battalion, Machine Gun Corps. Training Programme For Week Ending January 11th. 1919. App V	05/01/1919	05/01/1919
Miscellaneous	42nd Battalion, Machine Gun Corps. Training Programme For Week Ending January 18th. 1919. App VI	12/01/1919	12/01/1919
Miscellaneous	42nd. Battalion, Machine Gun Corps, Training Programme For Week Ending January 25th. 1919. App VII	19/01/1919	19/01/1919
Miscellaneous	42nd. Battalion, Machine Gun Corps. Training Programme For Week Ending February 1st. 1919. App VIII	25/01/1919	25/01/1919
Heading	(Original) War Diary of 42nd Battalion M.G.C. From 1.2.19 To 28.2.19 Volume I		
War Diary	Velaine	01/02/1919	28/02/1919
Miscellaneous	42nd. Battalion, Machine Gun Corps. Training Programme For Week Ending February 8th. 1919. App I	02/02/1919	02/02/1919
Heading	42nd Battalion M.G.C. War Diary for March 1919.		
War Diary	Velaine	01/03/1919	09/03/1919
War Diary	Montigny	10/03/1919	16/03/1919
War Diary	Velaine	17/03/1919	31/03/1919
Miscellaneous	H.Q. VI Corps.	06/06/1919	06/06/1919

Heading	War Diary 42nd. Bn. M.G. Corps. May 1st. 1919. to May 31st 1919.		
War Diary	Mungersdorf	01/05/1919	31/05/1919
Miscellaneous	Commandant, VI Corps Troops.	03/07/1919	03/07/1919
Heading	Original War Diary. 42nd Battalion. Machine Gun Corps. June 1919.		
War Diary	Mungersdorf	01/06/1919	30/06/1919

WO 95
2650/5

42ND DIVISION

42 BN MACHINE GUN CORPS

268TH MACHINE GUN COY.

JAN 1918-JUN 1919

WAR DIARY
or
INTELLIGENCE SUMMARY.

Army Form C. 2118.

42 Div
VOL I

WAR DIARY

268th M.G. Coy

Vol 1 Pages 1-3

CONFIDENTIAL

Jan 1918

WAR DIARY
INTELLIGENCE SUMMARY
(Erase heading not required.)

268 M.G. Coy

Army Form C. 2118.

Place	Date	Hour	Summary of Events and Information	Remarks and references to Appendices
GRANTHAM	1918 Jan 13		Coy entrain at GRANTHAM. Coy had been formed at the end of October under the command of Capt J D Gawthorpe to two command was handed over to Capt W.S. Bateman.	

Personnel

Coy Commander — CAPT W.F. DICKSON. at Res. Fus. attd M.G.C.
2nd in Command — CAPT C.A.M. JACKSON. M.G.C.

No. 1 Section — LT R.C.R. ALLERTON. M.G.C.
2LT J.R.S. GOULD. M.G.C.

No. 2 Section — LT J.R. BEECH. (Transport) M.G.C.
LT J.K. MICHELL. M.G.C.

No. 3 Section — LT G.S. MACINTOSH. 5th Seaforths attd M.G.C.
2LT F.S. HATCH. 4th Essex

No. 4 Section — LT G.F. ASHTON. M.G.C.
2LT J.R. GARDINER. M.G.C.
CSM Rose and No
177 other ranks including No
CQMS White.

During period between formation and today Coy has been under training at BELTON PARK GRANTHAM. Training had culminated with a Feb via BINGHAM, where a halt was made for the night of Dec 27. To TILSTHORPE Ave the Coy was billeted with 266, 267, and 269 Coys in the Reichsbankhaupt

Army Form C. 2118.

268 M.G. Coy (1)

WAR DIARY
or
INTELLIGENCE SUMMARY.
(Erase heading not required.)

Instructions regarding War Diaries and Intelligence Summaries are contained in F.S. Regs., Part II. and the Staff Manual respectively. Title pages will be prepared in manuscript.

Place	Date	Hour	Summary of Events and Information	Remarks and references to Appendices
	January		Training was carried out in fine weather being and Tactical schemes on Jan 4th. Coy returned to BINGHAM and on Jan 5th to BELTON PARK on Jan 9th the Coy was inspected by the G.O.C. M.G. T.C.	
SOUTHAMPTON	Jan 14		Entrained SOUTHAMPTON DOCKS. Embarked H.M.T. NIRVANAH	105P
HAVRE	Jan 15		Disembarked HAVRE 11.30 a.m. Crossing of channel without incident	105P
	16		Marched to No 1 Rest Camp. Arrived in darkness and rain	105P
	17		One day Coy inspection and camp fatigues	105P
	18		Camp fatigues.	
	19		Marched to GARE DES MARCHANDISES. Entrained. Train left 4.7 pm	105P
BETHUNE	20		Arrived BETHUNE 8.30 a.m. Detrained. Marched to billets at	105P
LOCON			LOCON. Coy joined with journey. Met at station by Officer from 125 M.G. Coy Coy inspection and Training. Returns by Dr Qm & Officers	105P
	21		4 In C Cos and Sw men attached to 126 & 127 M.G. Coys. Officers	
	22		remaining CUINCHY - FESTUBERT sector.	
	23		Elementary Training	105P
	24		Party attached to 126 & 127 M.G. Coy; return accidentally wounded	105P

WAR DIARY or INTELLIGENCE SUMMARY.

(Erase heading not required.)

Army Form C. 2118.

168 M.G. Coy (3)

Place	Date	Hour	Summary of Events and Information	Remarks and references to Appendices
LOCON	Jan 25		Fatigues	105P
	Jan 26		Party of men attached to 126 & 127 M.G. Coys returned.	105P
	Jan 27		No. 3 section relieve section of 125 M.G. Coy at CAILLOUX KEEP. Gun teams & S.O.S. barrages from A.9 & 5.2 to A.9.d.7.9 and to put down.	P.O.P.
			Church parades, gun cleaning.	
	28		Men attached to 126, 127 M.G. Coys on Return.	105P
	29		Elementary Training. Preparing for line.	105P
	30		Nos. 1 & 4 sections take over following positions in VILLAGE LINE. No. 1 CAMBRIN DEFENCES Nos 11 (A20.d.50.30), 9.14 (A20.c.70.35), P.F.1 (A16.d.4.6) P.F.11 (A14.b.10.15)	105P
	31		No.14 LEPS 5 (A8.a.35.95) LEPS 6 (A5&8.68) MGV 7 (A8.c.95.85) MG's & 6 Guns of No.4 section fired 750 rounds harassing fire on to Tank A.4.S.17. 067 moved from P.F.1 km A at all from line. Trench Mortar bombs in some Together on East night. Kounds 750	105P

WAR DIARY
or
INTELLIGENCE SUMMARY.

(Erase heading not required.)

Army Form C. 2118.

263rd MACHINE GUN COMPANY.

WAR DIARY
—
268th M.G. Coy
—
Vol 1. Papers 4-6

Feb 1st – Feb 28th 1918

CONFIDENTIAL

Place	Date	Hour	Summary of Events and Information	Remarks and references to Appendices

WAR DIARY
or
INTELLIGENCE SUMMARY
(Erase heading not required.)

Army Form C. 2118.

268th MACHINE GUN COMPANY.

No..........
Date..........

Instructions regarding War Diaries and Intelligence Summaries are contained in F.S. Regs., Part II. and the Staff Manual respectively. Title pages will be prepared in manuscript.

Place	Date 1918	Hour	Summary of Events and Information	Remarks and references to Appendices
GORRE	Feb. 1		Coy. H.Q. here with No 2 section to TUNING FORK ROAD. GORRE carried out at all positions A4 a 2-7. 1000 rounds harassing fire onto A4 a 2-7.	LA BASSEE 1:10000 36CNW / BETHUNE 1:40000
	2		Harassing fire. 1000 rounds on A4 a 2-7. 1500 rounds on A29 a 05·85. Considerable enemy activity, wiring and repairing all positions, our barrage set at CAILLOUX KEEP completed.	
	3		1000 rounds on A4 c 17.67. 1500 rounds onto CAMBRIN - LE FAUBOURG ROAD about A23 a 4.6. work at all positions	
	4		1500 rounds on A23 c 00.55. 1500 rounds on A4 c 17.67. work continued at all positions. Short heavy bombardment to the S. of Div. front between 8pm and 9pm.	
	5		No 2 section relieve No 3 section at CAILLOUX KEEP. 1500 rounds on talk and trench tramway between A4 d 40.85 and A4 a 55.25. 1500 rounds on band tinspatk at A16 d 65 45. Sniping all day.	
	6		Usual work. 1500 rounds at CAILLOUX KEEP. 1500 rounds onto A23 a 4 6. 1500 rounds onto A4 a 5·7	
	7		1500 rounds onto A23 a 4 4. 1500 rounds onto A4 c 08 92.	
	8		1500 rounds onto A23 c 40·16. 1500 rounds onto A4 d 3.5	
	9		1500 rounds onto A23 c 00 55. 1500 rounds onto trench between A4 B3.8 and A4 B 6.05	

WAR DIARY or INTELLIGENCE SUMMARY

268th MACHINE GUN COMPANY.

Place	Date	Hour	Summary of Events and Information	Remarks and references to Appendices
	10		Raid ordered for this evening cancelled. 2000 rounds into A 23 a 4.6 1500 rounds onto tracks between A 4 d 40.85 and A 4 a 85.25. Usual work.	108P
	11		One other rank wounded. A raiding party from the 1/26th Bn Btln entered enemy's line between A 3 d 43 90 and A 3 d 51 65. Raid was supported by fire from guns at CAILLOUX KEEP on to a line between A 9 b 55.15 and A 10 a 05.40. 9000 rounds were fired. Harassing fire to R. places before the raid on to KuK between A 4 d 40 85 and A 4 a 85 25 and during the raid 2000 rounds were fired on to A 23 c 40 16. work as usual.	108P
LA BEUVRIERE	12		Relieved by 196th M G Coy 6a relief coy marched to billett at LA BEUVRIERES. Relief complete 4.35 p.m.	108P
	13		Settling down in billets. Gleaning up.
	14		Section parade for Coy Commander's inspection. Bathing.
	15		Church Parade in billets. In billets at LAREUVRIERE are Nos 105, 106, and 107 M.G. Bry's. Under new organization for M.G.C. these from the Bry's of the Division will be formed into a Battalion under the command of Lt. Col. Tillin. the formation of the Battalion coy's are being formed under his orders. Training and football

WAR DIARY or INTELLIGENCE SUMMARY

265th MACHINE GUN COMPANY — Army Form C. 2118.

Place	Date	Hour	Summary of Events and Information	Remarks and references to Appendices
LA BEUVRIÈRE	Feb 16		Inspection of Coy by Lt Col Tillie	
	17		Church Parade. Fine day	
	18		Training continued. Coy parade by sections for instruction by Lt Irish Devlin in P.T. and bayonet fighting. Demonstration of barrage drill by No 1 section.	
	19		Demonstration of barrage drill by No 2 M.G. Coy and pack saddlery by No 4 section	
	20		Training in morning. Demonstration of steady drill by No 3	
	21		Section February. Coy football team play team from Field ambulance. Demonstration of gun mounting by No 12 section.	
	22		Training in morning. Football match against 105 M.G. Coy	
	23		Resting in morning. Recreation	
	24		Church Parade	
	25		Elementary Training. P.T. Lecture by Major General Solly Flood C.M.G. D.S.O. Infantry football team continued v. attacks Reg't	
	26		Pack Saddlery by Lt to the men continued of 113 M.G. Coy	
	27		C.A.M. Jackson horse Coy. Football in afternoon.	
	28		Elementary Training. Football by Lt Col Tillie	

42nd BATTALION, MACHINE GUN CORPS.

M A R C H

1 9 1 8

Attached:-

Appendices 1, 2, 3 & 4.

CONFIDENTIAL

ORIGINAL

WAR DIARY

OF

42ND BATTALION MACHINE GUN CORPS

FROM 1-3-18   TO 31-3-18

(VOLUME I)

Army Form C. 2118.

WAR DIARY
or
INTELLIGENCE SUMMARY.
(Erase heading not required.)

Instructions regarding War Diaries and Intelligence Summaries are contained in F. S. Regs., Part II. and the Staff Manual respectively. Title pages will be prepared in manuscript.

Place	Date	Hour	Summary of Events and Information	Remarks and references to Appendices
LABEUVRIERE	1-3-18		Battalion at LABEUVRIERE. Weather poor at intervals, visibility poor	
LABEUVRIERE	2-3-18		12th & Coy occupied LETOURET - BOUT - DELVILLE line	APPENDIX 1
			Very cold, snow fell, visibility very poor	
LABEUVRIERE	3-3-18		Frosty, visibility good	
LABEUVRIERE	4-3-18		Heavy thaw at intervals - visibility poor	
FOUQUIÈRES	5-3-18		H.Q. 12/5th, 12/6th and 12/7th Coys move to billets in FOUQUIÈRES, move completed by noon.	
			2/6 & Coy remains at LABEUVRIERE. Fair, strong wind, visibility good	
FOUQUIÈRES	6-3-18		Excellent visibility, very hot	
FOUQUIÈRES	7-3-18		Misty early, later sun shone, very mild	
FOUQUIÈRES	8-3-18		Reconnaissance of I Corps front (new positions) and methods of approach	
			Ground went sodden, sun shone all day, visibility excellent	
FOUQUIÈRES	9-3-18		Reconnaissance as on 8-3-18 completed. Sunny, visibility excellent. Snow announced 1 hour at 11 P.M.	
FOUQUIÈRES	10-3-18	3.5 PM	Battalion ordered to be in readiness to move at 12 hours notice (Wire G361)	
			Mostly cloudy, very mild, sunny, visibility excellent	
FOUQUIÈRES	11-3-18		Further reconnaissance of I Corps front (new positions) and approaches	
			Frosty, good visibility	
FOUQUIÈRES	12-3-18		Heavy rain early, sunny, visibility moderate	

Army Form C. 2118.

WAR DIARY
or
INTELLIGENCE SUMMARY.

(Erase heading not required.)

Instructions regarding War Diaries and Intelligence Summaries are contained in F. S. Regs., Part II. and the Staff Manual respectively. Title pages will be prepared in manuscript.

Place	Date	Hour	Summary of Events and Information	Remarks and references to Appendices
FOUQUIÈRES	13-3-18		Mild, visibility moderate.	CCR
FOUQUIÈRES	14-3-18		Heavy rain at intervals, fine later, cloudy, visibility poor.	CCR
FOUQUIÈRES	15-3-18	1-30 a.m.	125th Coy ordered to be in readiness to move at 2 hours notice by Wire (GS.129/6)	CCR
		10·49 a.m.	Wire (G.412) received stating 126th Coy no longer at 2 hours notice. Frosty, sunny, visibility excellent.	CCR
FOUQUIÈRES	16-3-18		Designation of Coys altered; 125th Coy to "A" Coy: 126th Coy to "B" Coy: 127th Coy to "C" Coy: 128th Coy to "D" Coy. Sunny all day, very mild, excellent visibility.	CCR CCR
FOUQUIÈRES	17-3-18		Fine, good visibility.	CCR
FOUQUIÈRES	18-3-18		LABEUVRIÈRE shelled during morning: casualties nil. Excellent visibility, warm & sunny.	CCR
FOUQUIÈRES	19-3-18		Fine early, rain later, visibility bad.	CCR
FOUQUIÈRES	20-3-18		Rainy, visibility poor	CCR
FOUQUIÈRES	21-3-18		Sun shone, visibility excellent.	CCR
FOUQUIÈRES	22-3-18		Dull, visibility poor	CCR
			During period 1-3-18 to 22-3-18 training as per attached appendix was carried out	APPENDIX II
			Orders received from Division to entrain the following day. All surplus stores were dumped at VAUDRICOURT	CCR
ADINFER WOOD	23-3-18		Battalion entrained at HESDIGNEUL carrying guns ammunition & equipment & two days rations & proceeded to ADINFER. All transport proceeded by road. Battalion less transport bivouaced for the night in ADINFER WOOD except C. Coy which proceeded to AYETTE with 12th Inf Bde & was held in immediate readiness.	CCR
	24-3-18	10·30 p.m.	Reconnaissance between by C.O. & Coy Comds of line BOIS-DE-LOGEAST — COURCELLES-LE-COMTE. Transport parked in of HAMEAU Farm.	CCR

Army Form C. 2118.

WAR DIARY
or
INTELLIGENCE SUMMARY.
(Erase heading not required.)

Instructions regarding War Diaries and Intelligence Summaries are contained in F. S. Regs., Part II. and the Staff Manual respectively. Title pages will be prepared in manuscript.

Place	Date	Hour	Summary of Events and Information	Remarks and references to Appendices
ADINFER WOOD	25.3.18	2.30 am	Whr ceased entering occupation of line from a point 1000 x S. of BOIS-DE-LOC EAST - Railway E. of COURCELLES-LE-COMTE. "A", "B" & "D" Coys ahead G., packed reinforces & moved to their position, which was organised in conjunction with infantry during the course of the day. Enemy attacks developed at ERVILLERS during the day. During the afternoon & day on the night went extend to throw back a dangerous right flank along the south edge of the BOIS-DE-LOC EAST during to enemy having entered ACHIET-LE-GRAND. Positions were taken up in conjunction with infantry in accordance with that order.	ccR
	26.3.18		Early in the morning information was received that the enemy had taken ACHIET-LE-PETIT and were moving to fall back on line BUCQUOY - ABLAINZEVELL. The M.Gs. assisted in covering the retirement. "A" Coy on right were attached to 127 Inf Bde.; "D" Coy on left to 126 Inf.Bde; "B" Coy were held in reserve and moved back to ESSARTS. "C" Coy lost connection with Battalion and fought a rearguard action back to AYETTE in area of 31st Division. Surplus stores were moved from ADINFER WOOD & ST AMAND and all second line transport proceeded to ST AMAND. Casualties Killed 2.O.R. Wounded 2/LIEUT R. METCALF (M.G.C) & 11 O.R. wounded at duty CAPT W.E DICKSON M.C. (H.Q. LANCS FUS). O.C. "D" Coy	ccR
FONQUEVILLERS	27.3.18		Batt. H.Q. moved to FONQUEVILLERS. Heavy fighting all along the line; enemy attacks several times but was driven off. M.Gs. obtained good targets & caused heavy casualties. FONQUEVILLERS shelled during day. Casualties Killed 2/Lieut A.T GRAHAM (M.G.C); 2/Lieut W. McRAE (M.G.C) and 5.O.R. Wounded 2/Lieut J.R.S. GOULD (M.G.C) & 39 O.R. wounded at duty Lieut A.L HERRIDGE (5th LANCS FUS) and 1 O.R.; Missing 15 O.R.	ccR

Army Form C. 2118.

WAR DIARY
or
INTELLIGENCE SUMMARY.
(Erase heading not required.)

Instructions regarding War Diaries and Intelligence Summaries are contained in F. S. Regs. Part II. and the Staff Manual respectively. Title pages will be prepared in manuscript.

Place	Date	Hour	Summary of Events and Information	Remarks and references to Appendices
ST AMAND	28-3-18		Battalion H.Q. moved to ST AMAND and all second line transport to COUIN. Heavy fighting. Enemy attacks everywhere on Divisional front were repulsed, but slight progress was made on front of 31st Div where "C" Coy were fighting. Communication was established with "C" Coy which was relieved by 31st Div during the night. "C" Coy on return proceeded to reliefs in ST AMAND. Casualties killed 3 O.R. wounded 1 O.R. wounded at duty 1 O.R.	C.e.R
	29-3-18		Less activity on the front. 42nd Div (also Artillery & M.G. Bath) was relieved by 4th Div during the course of the night 29/30 March. Casualties billed CAPT G.C. NAY (M.G.C.) O.C "A" Coy	C.e.R
	30-3-18		Enemy shelling; several local attacks were delivered by the enemy and broken off. A.B. & D Coys were relieved by 4th Div & moved to GOMMECOURT, ESSARTS and FONQUEVILLERS respectively with armn. Killed 4 O.R. wounded 2/Lieut R.W. MILLS (M.G.C.) & 6 O.R. Missing 1 O.R.	APPENDIX 3 C.e.R
	30-3-18		During the morning "C" Coy relieved "D" Coy in FONQUEVILLERS & "D" Coy moved to ST AMAND During the evening "C" Coy relieved "A" Coy in GOMMECOURT & "A" Coy moved to FONQUEVILLERS	Appendix 4 C.e.R

[signature]
LIEUT COL
COMDG 42nd Batt M.G.C.

APPENDICES

1, 2, 3 & 4.

Appendix I

Ref. Sheet – 36.A.S.E. 1/20,000

Occupation of LE TOURET-BOUT DELVILLE LINE on 2-3-18

by 126th M.G. Coy.

Wire (A) to "stand to" received at 6.45 A.M.
Wire (B) to occupy line received at 7.45 A.M.

4 Motor lorries arrived at 8.A.M. & 126th M.G. Coy. loaded up & proceeded at 8.45 A.M.

The guns were manned for action in the following positions at the following times

HUIT MAISON –
  R 29 b 60·30 10·10 a m
  R 29 b 95·50 10·10 a m
  R 23 a 80·20 10·10 am
  R 23 b 70·00 10·10 am.

LACOUTURE –
  X 5 a 20·80 10·30 am
  X 5 b 10·30 10·30 am
  X 5 c 90·80 10·30 am
  X 4 d 90·90 10·30 am

MESPLAUX. N. –
  X 8 b 50·20 10·30 am
  X 8 b 90·80 10·30 am

MESPLAUX. W. –
  X 14 d 90·30 10·30 am
  X 14 a 80·20 10·30 am

2 guns in Orchard about R 34 C 80·40 10·15 AM
2 guns about X 34 C 40·90   10·15 AM

Coy. H.Q. were established at Brigade H.Q. in ZELOBES at 9·45 am

Orders to return to billets received at 2·30 PM
Billets in LABEUVRIERE reached at 5.PM.
No ammunition expended. No Casualties

Sketch map attached (C) showing gun positions

Cause of occupation Owing to a German raiding party having broken into Portuguese front. The Portuguese later ejected the raiders

"C" Form.
MESSAGES AND SIGNALS.

Army Form C. 2123.
(In books of 100.)

Prefix **SB** Code **32** Words **68**

Service Instructions: Urgently

Handed in at **YDB** Received **6.45A** m

TO: **42 DMGO**

126th	Inf	Bde	and
126	MG Coy	will	stand
by	ready	to	occupy
LE	TOURET	BOUT.	Delville
line	aaa	Bde	&
DMGO	will	report	when
troops	are	ready	to
move	aaa	ECLEME	Battn
will	march	to at	once
to	CHOCQUES	and	will
be	met	by	lorries
at	V28 A8.2	aaa	lorries
are	being	sent	to
126	MG Coy	aaa	added
126	Inf	Bde	&
DMGO			

FROM PLACE & TIME: **42nd Division**

"C" Form.			Army Form C. 2123. (In books of 100.)
MESSAGES AND SIGNALS			No. of Message
Prefix Code Words 53	Received. From Arty	Sent, or sent out. At m	Office Stamp.
Charges to Collect	By Duty	To	
Service Instructions Urgent Priority		By	
Handed in at 7.05	Office 7.45 m.	Received 7.45 a.m	

TO 42 Div GO Labeuvrière

*Sender's Number	Day of Month.	In reply to Number	A A A
G259	3		

126 Inf Bde will relieve the LE TOURET DEL VILLAGE LINE at once aaa Lorries are being sent to LA BEUVRIERE to move up 126th MG Coy aaa 126th Inf Bde will report when in position aaa addsd 126th Inf Bde DivGO Reptd all concerned

FROM PLACE & TIME 42nd Divn

* This line should be erased if not required.

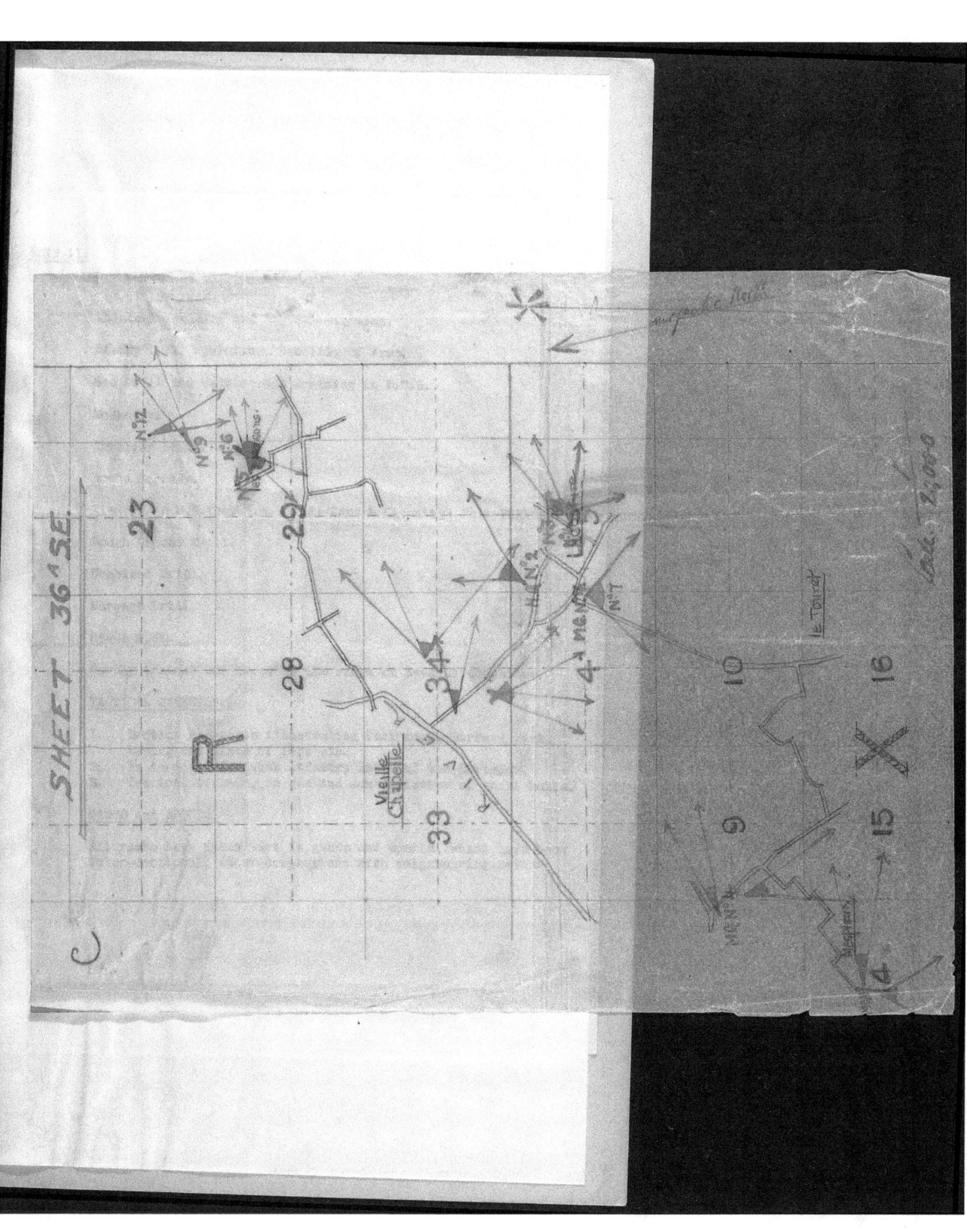

APPENDIX II.

TRAINING.

Physical Training and Bayonet Fighting.

Steady Drill, Saluting, Handling of Arms.

Gas Drill and Machine Gun Training in S.B.R.

Musketry.

Revolver Drill.

Route Marches.

Elementary M.G.Work i.e. I.A: Care & Cleaning: Belt Filling.

Rough Ground Drill.

Combined Drill.

Barrage Drill.

RANGE WORK.

Partly trained men fired on the range on several occasions.

TACTICAL EXERCISES.

1. Section exercises illustrating Pack work, Barrage work, Laying out lines of fire etc.
2. In co-operation with Infantry units of the Division.
3. Tactical training in use and consolidation of shell holes.

GAMES and SPORTS.

All ranks have taken part in games and sports, which have been inter-sectional, inter-company and with neighbouring units.

SECRET.   Copy No. 8   Appendix III

              42nd. Battalion, M.G.C. Order No. A.

                                                March 30th, 1918.

1.   A, B, and D. Companies, 42nd. Battalion, M.G.C. will be
      relieved by the 41st. Battalion, M.G.C. and a Composite M.G.
      squadron of 12 guns under Command of Major Peters tomorrow
      night, March 30/31st.

2.   B. Company (16 guns) will be relieved by a group of machine
      guns from 41st. Battalion, M.G.C.
      A. Company (12 guns) will be relieved by a group of machine
      guns from 41st. Battalion, M.G.C.
      D. Company will be relieved by the Composite Machine Gun
      Squadron.
      Details of relief to be arranged between O.Cs. concerned.

3.   Relieving guns will leave COURCELETTE by 6 p.m.

4.   Relief to be completed by 9 p.m. and reported to Battalion H.Q.

5.   On relief Companies will proceed to a destination to be
      notified later.

6.   ACKNOWLEDGE.

                                   C.Rose Capt. & Adjt.
DISTRIBUTION:-   42nd. Battalion, M.G.C.

Copies 1 to 3   A.B.& D. Coys.
   "   No. 4.   Composite M.G. Squadron.
   "   " 5.   41st. Division.
   "   " 6.   42nd. Division.
   "   " 7.   41st. M.G.Bn.
   "   " 8 & 9. War Diary

Appendix III

SECRET.   Copy No...8...

Reference Operation Order No.4.

Companies will proceed on relief to the following destinations:-

    A. Company. - FONQUEVILLERS.

    B.   "   - PURPLE LINE and will be under orders of
                       G.O.C. 126th. Infantry Brigade.
    D.   "   - GOMMECOURT and will be under orders of
                       G.O.C. 127th. Infantry Brigade.

Distribution
As Operation Order
No.4.
                            CCRose
                                Capt. & Adjt.
                            42nd. Battalion, M.G.C.

29/3/18.

Appendix IV

SECRET.   Copy No............4......

42nd. Battalion: M.G.C. Order No.1.
                                                         March 30th. 1918.

1. C. Company will relieve D. Company in FONQUEVILLERS by
    noon tomorrow. O.C. 'C' Company will arrange a previous
    reconnaissance.

2. A guard will be left over C. Company's billets.

3. On relief D. Company will move to ST AMAND and take over
    billets vacated by C. Company.

4. On the evening of the 31/1st. C. Company will relieve A. Company
    in GOMMECOURT.

5. On relief A. Company will move to FONQUEVILLERS and take over
    billets vacated by C. Company.

6. Completion of reliefs to be notified to Battalion H.Q.

7. ACKNOWLEDGE.

                              C C Rose.   Capt & Adjt.
                                  42nd. Battalion, Machine Gun Corps.

DISTRIBUTION.
Copies 1 to 3 to
        A, C, & D. Coy s.
     " No. 4 & 5. War Diary.

42nd Div.
IV.Corps.

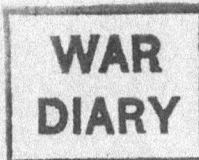

42nd BATTALION, MACHINE GUN CORPS.

A P R I L

1 9 1 8

Attached:

Appendices I, II, III,
IV, V, VI & VII.

CONFIDENTIAL

ORIGINAL

WAR DIARY

OF

42ND BATTALION MACHINE GUN CORPS.

(VOLUME II)

From 1-4-18.   To 30-4-18.

42ND BATTALION,
MACHINE GUN
CORPS.

No. M.G./272.
Date 2.5.18.

WAR DIARY
or
INTELLIGENCE SUMMARY.
(Erase heading not required.)

Army Form C. 2118.

Instructions regarding War Diaries and Intelligence Summaries are contained in F. S. Regs., Part II. and the Staff Manual respectively. Title pages will be prepared in manuscript.

Place	Date	Hour	Summary of Events and Information	Remarks and references to Appendices
ST AMAND	1-4-18		Cloudy early, Sun later, visibility fair. During the night 1/2 42nd Divn (Rear artillery) relieved 41st Divn (Rear artillery). 4.1st Battn M.G.C ("A" Coy) relieved 4.1st Battn M.G.C in the Left Sector IV Corps front. Dispositions "B" Coy Right Sector, "C" Coy Left Sector, "D" Coy Support. Relief completed "B" Coy at 2.30 AM. "C" Coy at 3.30 AM, "D" Coy at 5.30 AM. Casualties Wounded 2 O.R.	APP. I CCR
	2-4-18		Sunny, visibility good, heavy rain during evening. Transport moved from COUIN to SOUASTRE move completed by 10 AM. Situation on our front quiet, intermittent shelling of back areas, particularly around ESSARTS. At dusk "A" Coy 142nd Battn M.G.C relieved Composit M.G Squadron. Relief completed at 11 P.M. Casualties Wounded 1 O.R. Missing 1 O.R.	APP II CCR
	3-4-18	7 AM	Dull + showery, visibility bad. 2/Lieut BARNETT (B Coy) captured an enemy messenger dog at the crossing BUCQUOY. Two messages were taken off collar + forwarded to 126th Inf Bde intelligence Officer, who states they contained important information. Enemy artillery active during day shelling front line + back areas, particularly ESSARTS and vicinity. 8 P.M. to 10 P.M. artillery very active, enemy barrage fell along BUCQUOY - AYETTE road. Enemy aircraft active early in day, several went dropped on a battery of artillery behind M.G. carried out indirect Sht on road running through F21b during night. Starving gun of our M.G. was accurately enfilladed by machine portion. 5100 rds were fired into W.G. S.E. of ABLAINZEVELLE Casualties Wounded 1 O.R.	CCR
MENU	4-4-18		Intermittent rain all day, visibility bad. Reconnaissance + arrangements made to extend PURPLE LINE by O'sC Coys	

A 5834. Wt. W4973/M687 750,000 8/16 D. D. & L. Ltd. Forms/C.2118/13

WAR DIARY or INTELLIGENCE SUMMARY

Army Form C. 2118.

Place	Date	Hour	Summary of Events and Information	Remarks and references to Appendices
		3 P.M.	Battn. H.Q. moved to HENU.	
			Enemy artillery bombarded back areas with H.E. & gas shell intermittently all day. Bucquoy & ESSARTS heavily shelled. Strong artillery duel during evening. Enemy M.G. action during night sweeping area round Bucquoy. "B" coy M.G. fired 7000 to harassing fire during the night. "B" coy shot an enemy messenger dog at 3 P.M. either containing message or fastened to L1255 and 560. Casualties Wounded 2.O.R. wounded at duty 3.O.R	c/f
HENU	5-4-18		Dull, visibility bad	
			A successful local attack was carried out by the 37th Div. on our right. "D" coy co-operated with 4 guns, which harassed enemy line L.13 d 45.90 to L.13 b 99.90. Heavy fighting took place throughout the day in and around Bucquoy. On return mobile bombardment of H.E. & gas shells on front system & back areas commenced at 5.30 a.m. also a T.M. bombardment of front system which continued 2.08 "B" coys forward M.G. Enemy launched attack about 10 A.M. "B" coys remaining 2 forward guns fired about 1000 rds & were then disengaged. A counter attack was launched at 4.30 P.M. & our line was consolidated from 42.b.05 G.L.3.b.48 to original line at F.26.C.41. Enemy recapt ESSARTS Bucquoy road with M.G. fire during night "A"coy M.Gs. harassed enemy back areas during night 5,000 rds were fired.	
		1 P.M.	42nd Div (Warning) Order No 7 received saying Div would be relieved by 62nd Div on night 7/8 & 8/9 April. Casualties Missing 2/Lieut M.R. LEAMAN M.S.C. & 11.O.R. Killed 2.O.R. Wounded 14 O.R. Wounded & gas 21 O.R.	c/f
	6-4-18		Fine, sun shone, visibility fair. Heavy rain at night.	
		7.30 P.M.	During day ESSARTS & vicinity was shelled with 5.9 H.E. & 77 mm shrapnel & gas shells. 42nd Div Op. Order No 8 received & also administrative Instructions no 52. Casualties Killed 3.O.R. Wounded at duty 2.O.R.Wounded Gas 5.O.R.	
	7-4-18		Wet, cold, misted hailstorm, visibility bad	
		9.30 A.M.	Enemy infantry were seen advancing from Gomm ... Bucquoy from the ridge on the Eastern side. M.G.	

Army Form C. 2118.

WAR DIARY
or
INTELLIGENCE SUMMARY.

(Erase heading not required.)

Instructions regarding War Diaries and Intelligence Summaries are contained in F. S. Regs., Part II. and the Staff Manual respectively. Title pages will be prepared in manuscript.

Place	Date	Hour	Summary of Events and Information	Remarks and references to Appendices
HENU	7-4-18		Barrage balloons fired on S.O.S. No attacks were launched from enemy front line, so it is assumed that enemy was not reporting own Ck open. Enemy was dispersed.	
			Situation quiet otherwise. Essarts shelled intermittently during day.	
			Casualties wounded 2 O.R.	cfR
		11 a.m	Reconnaissance of front by Coy. Commanders of 62nd Batt. M.G.C. during the day.	
AUTHIE	8-4-18		Enemy actively during morning replied to intermittent shelling	
		2 p.m.–5 p.m	Enemy shelled back area with 5.9's	
			Was early, visibility bad	
			Batt. H.Q. moved to AUTHIE, move completed by 6.30 p.m. All transport & stores moved during day to AUTHIE	APP III
			Relief of 42nd Batt. M.G.C. by 62nd Batt. M.G.C. commenced at dusk. Coys. in relief embussed at SOUASTRE and proceeded to billets in AUTHIE. Casualties 1 O.R.	cfR
	9-4-18		Relief completed at 6.30 a.m	cfR
			Day was devoted to rest, baths, cleaning & overhauling guns & equipment.	
	10-4-18	2 a.m	Wire received from 42nd Div ordering Battalion G to be in readiness to move at half an hours notice between 5 a.m. and 9 a.m.	
			Day early, dull & after windy very bad	
			Day devoted to baths, cleaning & overhauling guns & equipment & resting	
			Reconnaissance to RED LINE and recently by C.O. & O's Commanding Coys	cfR

Army Form C.2118.

WAR DIARY
or
INTELLIGENCE SUMMARY.
(Erase heading not required.)

Army Form C. 2118.

Place	Date	Hour	Summary of Events and Information	Remarks and references to Appendices
AUTHIE	11-4-18		Fine, warm, sun about all day, visibility good	
			Training, Physical training and bayonet fighting was carried out by all Coys during the morning	CCR
			Battalion was inspected by G.O.C. 142nd Division during the afternoon	
			A further reconnaissance of the RED LINE was carried out	
	12-4-18		Fine, warm, sunny, visibility excellent	
			All Coys carried out P.T. & B.F. & also had baths	
			The reconnaissance of the RED LINE & approaches was continued, by Coy Commanders & Section Officers	CCR
		11.30 AM	Orders received from 142nd Div. that all Coys must be clear of AUTHIE by 5 P.M. 14-4-18	CCR
	13-4-18		Dull, mild, visibility poor. P.T. & B.F. were carried out	
			The reconnaissance of the RED LINE was continued.	
	14-4-18		Very cold, strong east wind, visibility poor	
		4 A.M	All Coys & transport moved to the vicinity of the BOIS du WARNIMONT. The move was completed at 5 A.M.	CCR
COUIN			Battalion H.Q. moved to COUIN. The move was completed at 6 A.M.	
		7 AM	"B", "C" Coys proceeded to their allotted position in the RED LINE and also conveyed S.A.A from Dumps & placed it in the vicinity of the gun positions. After the Meal was carried out "B" & "C" Coys returned to their bivouacs in the vicinity of the BOIS du WARNIMONT.	
		7.30 PM	Read Div. Order No 10 received, also administrative instruction no 54	CCR
	15-4-18		Windy, cold, visibility bad	
			P.T. and B.F. was carried out during the course of the day by all Coys.	
			A, B, C & D Coys during the early afternoon marched back again into billets in AUTHIE.	CCR

Army Form C. 2118.

WAR DIARY
or
INTELLIGENCE SUMMARY.
(Erase heading not required.)

Instructions regarding War Diaries and Intelligence Summaries are contained in F. S. Regs., Part II. and the Staff Manual respectively. Title pages will be prepared in manuscript.

Place	Date	Hour	Summary of Events and Information	Remarks and references to Appendices
COUIN	16-4-18		Cold & visibility poor, slight rain. All Coy carried out PT & BF & road walks.	c.R
	17-4-18		Fine early, rain later, visibility very bad. 1 Officer & 14 O.R. per Coy went to rest billet in COUIN. Hand Bott H.G.C. relieved 3/5 Batt M.G.C. in the entire sector IV Corps front during night 17/18 April. Dispositions "B" Coy on left, "C" Coy in centre, "D" Coy on right, "A" Coy in reserve. All transport & baths surplus moved to vicinity of COUIN. (J.2.c.) Casualties nil.	c.R APP III c.R
	18-4-18		Wet, visibility bad.	
		5 AM	2 Sections of "A" Coy moved up into positions, one section to J.24.a & the other to K.1 central from which positions they could if necessary sweep the ground between GOMMECOURT PARK and HEBUTERNE. Our M.Gs fired 1500 rds on K.15 & 25.95 during the night. Enemy artillery moderately quiet. Our artillery fired intermittently during day, but was very active at night a large amount of work was carried out on gun emplacements. Casualties Wounded 1.O.R. Wounded duty expected 1.O.R.	c.R
	19-4-18		Persistent hail & snow storms, between sun shone brightly & visibility was good. Our M.Gs fired 4700 rds on Sunken road & trench in L.13 a. & also 3000 rds in support of raids by 12.5 Bde fired in the form of a barrage assisting enfilade portion of artillery use barrage "A" Coy were withdrawn into reserve in wood J.2.C.&D. Move was completed by 6.30 P.M. enemy artillery active. Ours active particularly during the day. Enemy M.Gs swept our trenches in L.1.c, K.5d, K.6.c & GOMMECOURT PARK. Casualties nil	c.R

A5834 Wt. W4973/M687 750,000 8/16 D. D. & L. Ltd. Forms/C.2118/13

Army Form C. 2118.

WAR DIARY
or
INTELLIGENCE SUMMARY.
(Erase heading not required.)

Instructions regarding War Diaries and Intelligence Summaries are contained in F.S. Regs., Part II. and the Staff Manual respectively. Title pages will be prepared in manuscript.

Place	Date	Hour	Summary of Events and Information	Remarks and references to Appendices
COUIN	20-4-18		Fine, heavy showers at intervals, visibility moderate.	
			Our artillery very active during night. Enemy artillery moderately active.	
			Our M.Gs carried out harassing fire on tracks in K.18.a., Sunken road & trench in L.13.a., trenches at K.18 & 2.9 and S.E. edge of ROSSIGNOL WOOD, 14,200 rounds were fired.	
			Enemy M.Gs carried out a certain amount of sweeping fire during the night.	
			Work. Many slit and alternative emplacements were dug.	
			Casualties Killed 1.O.R. Wounded 1.O.R.	C.C.R.
	21-4-18		Bright, sunny, visibility moderate owing to haze.	
			Enemy artillery active. Ours very active especially during night.	
			Our M.Gs carried out harassing fire on same targets as 20-4-18, 14,000 rds were fired.	
			2 new emplacements were dug in K.5.d, 5 & a, considerable amount of work was done to existing emplacements	
			Casualties Killed 1.O.R. Wounded self inflicted 1.O.R.	C.C.R.
	22-4-18		Fine and sunny all day, visibility good, slight rain in evening	
			Enemy artillery active, Ours very active. Our M.Gs fired 15,000 rounds harassing fire on same targets as 20-4-18. Enemy M.G. very active fired in areas E.30.c. K.6.a & 15.d. and GOMMECOURT ROAD	
			Work. Several emplacements dug & camouflaged & S.A.A. & self tree shelters constructed, slit trenches & shelters made.	
			Casualties Wounded 2.O.R.	C.C.R.
	23-4-18		Fine, sunny, very mild, visibility good.	
			Situation quiet, no unusual activity.	
			Our M.Gs fired 15,500 rounds during the night in the usual targets.	
			Casualties nil.	C.C.R.

A.5834 Wt. W4973/M687 750,000 8/16 D.D. & L. Ltd. Forms/C.2118/13

WAR DIARY
or
INTELLIGENCE SUMMARY.
(Erase heading not required.)

Army Form C. 2118.

Place	Date	Hour	Summary of Events and Information	Remarks and references to Appendices
COUIN	24-4-18		Dull, showery, visibility poor owing to mist throughout the day. Enemy artillery quiet, ours very active 8 p.m – 10 p.m. Enemy shelled vicinity of COUIN about 6.30 p.m. Our M.Gs fired 13,500 rounds during the night on usual targets. Work improvements to gun positions & trenches generally. During the night "A" Coy relieved "B" Coy. Relief was completed at 4.45 A.M. 25/4/18. During the night 8 guns of "D" Coy 42nd Battn M.G.C. were relieved by New Zealand M.G. Battn. Relief was completed at 8.25 a.m. 25/4/18. Casualties 1 O.R. wounded.	APP V APP VI ccR
	25-4-18		Dull, visibility very low, rain at night. Our artillery moderately active specially at night. Enemy artillery very active from 8.30 p.m – 11 p.m retaliating on our trench system and back areas. Our M.Gs carried out harassing fire during the night on usual targets. 12,000 rds fired. Enemy M.Gs fired occasional bursts during the night. Work improvement of trenches in vicinity of guns & repairs to emplacements generally. Casualties nil.	ccR
	26-4-18		Very dull, mist early, visibility very low all day, frequent drizzling rain. Situation in front very quiet. Enemy M.Gs active at night, our M.Gs fired 11,500 rds on usual targets during the night. Improvements carried out to trenches & gun positions, several minor & automatic guns position commenced. Casualties nil.	ccR
	27-4-18		Very dull, visibility low, rain during evening. Situation on the front quiet. Our M.Gs fired 6,500 rounds harassing fire on the usual targets. Enemy M.Gs very active during the night especially in vicinity of GOMMECOURT WOOD. Work new emplacement constructed & improvements to emplacements generally. Casualties nil.	ccR

Army Form C. 2118.

8.

WAR DIARY
or
INTELLIGENCE SUMMARY.
(Erase heading not required.)

Instructions regarding War Diaries and Intelligence Summaries are contained in F.S. Regs., Part II. and the Staff Manual respectively. Title pages will be prepared in manuscript.

Place	Date	Hour	Summary of Events and Information	Remarks and references to Appendices
COUIN	28-4-18		Dull, visibility very bad. Situation quiet, artillery very active during enemy & night. Enemy M.Gs very active during the night sweeping our trench system, roads & tracks. Our M.Gs fired 4,500 rds. harassing fire on usual targets. Work: Improvements & repairs to trenches and gun positions generally. Continuation of construction of new positions and S.A.A. nullur. "B" Coy on relief relieved the 6 guns of "D" Coy in the right group. The relief Coy on relief proceeded to bivouacs at T.2.d.0.4. which was completed at 1 A.M. Casualties nil. Our visibility poor, wet at night.	C.R.
	30-4-18		Our artillery very active throughout the day & night; enemy artillery was more active than usual. Our M.Gs fired 16,500 rounds harassing fire on usual targets. Information was received that an enemy relief was in progress in trench K 12.a. Fire was immediately opened by on of our M.Gs & the shots were observed falling in the trench & the enemy were seen to scatter. Enemy M.Gs were very active between 8.15 p.m & 11 p.m. Work: Several new positions & shelters were completed & usual improvement continued. Casualties nil.	C.R.
			Dull, visibility very low, steady rain during morning. Situation in morning quiet. Our M.Gs fired 6000 rounds harassing fire on usual targets. Enemy M.Gs were very active during the night. "B" Coy 42nd Battn M.G.C. relieved "C" Coy 42nd Battn M.G.C during the night 30/1st May. Relief was completed at 4 am 1st May and "C" Coy proceeded to bivouacs at T.2.d.0.4. Casualties Wounded 1 O.R. Wounded at duty 1 O.R.	APP VII C.R.

W.H. Lee
Lieut Col
Cmg. 42nd Batt. M.G.C

APPENDICES

I, II, III, IV, V, VI

& VII.

SECRET.   APP. I   Copy No. 11

42nd. Battalion, M.G.C. Order No. 7.

March 31st. 1918.

1. The 42nd. Battalion, M.G.C. will relieve the 41st. Battalion, M.G.C. in Left Sector of IV Corps Front on night 1/2nd. April.

2. C. Company will co-operate with G.O.C. 188th. Inf. Brigade H.Qrs. ESSARTS and will be responsible for placing a barrage of 4 guns on Northern Edge of ABLAINZEVELLE near F.23.Central. Arrangements to observe the area in F.23.b. and F.17.b. and d. will be made.

3. B. Company will co-operate with G.O.C. 125th. Inf. Brigade, H.Qrs. ESSARTS and will be responsible for placing a barrage of 4 guns on Southern Edge of ABLAINZEVELLE and hutments in F.29.b. & F.23.d.

4. D. Company will co-operate with G.O.C. 127th. Inf. Brigade, H.Qrs. ESSARTS and will be responsible for having a 4 gun battery near L.2.b.2.2. which can fire South and S.E. and command the ground near L.2.Central.
   The remaining guns of D. Company will be disposed:-
   (a) So as to bring fire to bear on BUCQUOY-ABLAINZEVELLE RIDGE.
   (b) So as to give depth to the defence of the Sector.

5. A. Company will be in Reserve.

6. The M.G.Squadron will remain in position near F.26.C.Central and will continue to maintain 12 Machine Guns laid on a barrage line from L.9.b.9.5. to L.10.a.3.8.

7. Relief to be completed by 6am. 2nd. April.

8. All Maps to be handed over.

9. Completion of relief and location of H.Qrs. of Companies to be reported to M.G.Battalion H.Qrs. which will not move.

10. ACKNOWLEDGE.

Distribution.
Copies 1 to 4. A.B.C.& D.Coys.
"   " No. 5. 125th. Inf. Brigade
"   "   " 6. 126th. "   "
"   "   " 7. 127th. "   "
"   "   " 8. 41st. M.G.Bn.
"   "   " 9. M.G.Squadron.
"   "   " 10. File.
"   "   " 11 & 12. War Diary.

cc Rose
Capt. & Adjt.
42nd. Battalion, M.G.C.

APP II

42nd. Battalion, M.G.C. Order No. 8.

Copy No..... 4......

April 1st. 1918.

SECRET.

1. A. Company (1/5) 42nd. Battalion, M.G.C. will relieve the Composite M.G. Squadron commanded by Major Waters at dusk on the 2nd. instant.
Headquarters of Composite M.G. Squadron is at E.24.b.1.0.
10 guns will be sent up to relieve the Machine Gun Squadron.

2. The battery positions and barrage lines of the Composite M.G.Squadron will be taken over and maintained.

3. On relief the Composite M.G.Squadron will move to HARIFUX and report arrival to Corps Headquarters.

4. A. Company (1/5) 42nd. Battalion, M.G.C. will take over the H.Qrs. from the Composite M.G.Squadron maintaining a rear H.Qrs. at RONQUEVILLERS.

5. Completion of relief to be reported to Battalion H. Qrs.

6. ACKNOWLEDGE.

C.Rose Capt. & Adjt.
42nd. Battalion. M.G.C.

Distribution.
Copy No. 1. A Coy (1/5)
  "   " 2. Composite M.G. Squadron.
  "   " 3. 127th. Infy. Brigade.
  "   " 4 & 5. War Diary.
  "   " 6. File

A.P.P. IV

WARNING ORDER.

April. 14th. 1918.

COPY NO......6...

1. The 42nd. Battalion, M.G.C. will relieve the 37th. Battalion, M.G.C. in the Centre Sector, IV Corps Front, on the night 17/18th. April.

2. O.C. B. C. and D. Companies with section officers will reconnoitre the Northern, Centre, and Southern Sectors respectively on the morning of the 16th. instant.

3. The H.Qrs. of the Company of the 37th. Bn. M.G.C. to be relieved by B. Company, 42nd. Bn. M.G.C. is at E.29.d.10.80.
The H.Qrs. of the Company of the 37th. Bn. M.G.C. to be relieved by C. Company is at E.23.d.10.80.
The H.Qrs. of the Company of the 37th. Bn. M.G.C. to be relieved by D. Company is at K.3.c.45.10.

4. The 42nd. Division will be on a 3 Brigade Front in the line, with 126th. Inf. Bde. on the North, 127th. Inf. Bde. in the Centre, and 125th. Inf. Bde. in the South.

5. One Officer and 5 O.R. per Company will go on in advance and will report at the H.Qrs. of the Company being relieved at dawn on the 17th instant.

6. More detailed orders will follow.

7. ACKNOWLEDGE.

W.Ross Capt. & Adjt.
42nd. Battalion, M.G.C.

Distribution.
Copies 1 to 4. A.B.C. & D. Coys.
" No. 5. 37th. Bn. M.G.C.
" " 6 & 7. War Diary.
" " 8. File.

APP IV

SECRET.   Copy No...7.....

42nd. Battalion, M.G.C. Order No. 11.

April 15th. 1918.

In continuation of Warning Order dated 14th. instant:-

1. The four Companies of 42nd. Battalion, M.G.C. will vacate their present camp and will proceed to relieve the 37th. Battalion, M.G.C. at 12.30 p.m. on 17th. instant.
    B. Company will lead followed by C. D. and A. Companies
    The march will be by sections. 200 yards interval will be maintained between sections, and 500 yards interval will be maintained between Companies.

2. A. Company will proceed to H. Qrs. at J.2.b.7.5. and will relieve the Company of the 37th. Battalion, M.G.C. in reserve there.

3. A. Company will be distributed as follows:-
    10 guns near J.2.b.7.5. in reserve.
    4 guns near K.1.c.8.8. (astride road)
    2 guns near K.7.c.5.3.
    This is the disposition of the guns of the Company of the 37th. Battalion, M.G.C. at present in reserve.

4. Officers Commanding B. C. and D. Companies will select staging areas West of the line CHATEAU de la HAIE - SAILLY-au-BOIS.
    (a) The staging areas of Companies will be at least 800 yards apart.
    (b) Companies will march to the selected staging area by sections (each section complete with transport).
    (c) Dinners or teas will be provided in the staging area and Companies will not move from staging areas to relieve in the trenches until dusk, unless visibility is very bad.

5. Company Sergeant Majors will be responsible for knowing the total amount of S.A.A. in machine gun positions or machine gun reserve positions in the Company area.
    A considerable quantity of S.A.A. will be handed over.

6. All maps, range cards, programmes of work, barrage charts will be handed over.

7. Forward Divisional Report Centre will be at FONQUEVILLERS Church.

8. It is proposed to put Forward Battalion H.Qrs. in dugout at E.28.d.10.80 and O.C. B. Company is warned that his Company H.Qrs. will probably have to move to old Company H.Q. dugout at K.5.b.1.7. which ought to be reconnoitred tomorrow.

9. The attached tracing shows how the guns of the 42nd. Bn. M.G.C. will be distributed after relief. The only change is that C. Company takes over the 4 guns at K.5.a. Nos. 26, 27, 28 and 29. which were in B. Company's Sector according to 37th. Division Defence Scheme.

10. ACKNOWLEDGE.

Distribution.
Copies 1 to 4. A.B.C.& D.Coys.
  " No. 5. 37th. Bn. M.G.C.
  "   " 6. H.Q. 42nd. Division.
  "   " 7 & 8. War Diary.
  "   " 9. File.
  "   " 10,11,12. 125th, 126th, 127th Inf. Bdes.

c.c.Rose
Capt.& Adjt.
42nd. Battalion, M.G.C.

APP V   Copy No......7...

ORDER.

42nd. Battalion, H.C.S. Order No. 1.   April 24th, 1915.

1. A Company, 42nd. Battalion, H.C.S. will relieve B Company, 42nd. Battalion, H.C.S. by dawn on April 25th.

2. All arrangements will be made between Company Commanders concerned.

3. On relief B Company will proceed to bivouacs in vicinity of J.2.d.0.4.

4. Completion of relief will be notified by code word "NELSON"

5. ACKNOWLEDGE.

Distribution.
Copy No. 1. A Company.
  "   "   2. B   "
  "   "   3. H.Q. 184th Inf. Bde.
  "   "   4. H.Q. 62nd Division.
  "   "   5. 17 Corps H.Q. Officer.
  "   "   6 & 7. War Diary.
  "   "   8. File.

M.K. Rice
Lieut-Colonel,
Cmdg. 42nd. Battalion, H.C.S.

App VI

SECRET

17th Battalion, H.Q. O. Order No. 17 Aug 24 1918

On the night of 25th April, 1918, C Company at present in the line will be relieved by B Company of the 1st Battalion of the New Zealand Division. All arrangements will be made direct between Company Commanders. B Company will take over the present role of C Company.

On relief the C Coy of D Company will rendezvous near the line, and proceed at once when passed to J.2.d.0.4.

Rolls will be reported on arrival by O.C. who will command.

Zero hour .30.

C C Rose
Capt. Adjt, 17th Batty. H.Q.

Distribution   Copies
1. O. Bayer Rank   .
2. O. A Coy H.Q.   .
3. IV Coy H.Q. Tempe .
4. C Coy H.Q. Report .
5. O.C. No 1 Coy   .
6. O.C. No 2 Coy   .
7. O.C. No 3 Coy   .
8. File   .

APP VII

Copy No............

SECRET.
42nd. Battalion, M.G.C. Order No. 14.
April 29th, 1918.

1. D. Company, 42nd. Battalion, M.G.C. will relieve C. Company 42nd. Battalion, M.G.C. on the morning 1st. May at dawn. O.C. D. Coy. will then become O.C. Right Group of Machine Guns affiliated to 127th Inf. Bde.

2. An advance party of One Officer and 5 O.Rs. will report to O. Company H.Qrs. on the evening of the 30th.

3. All Maps, Range Cards, Programmes of Work, Barrage Charts etc. will be handed over.

4. Machine Gun S.A.A. Dumps will be carefully checked and handed over.

5. On relief C. Company will take over camp vacated by D. Company at J.2.6.0.4.

6. Completion of relief will be reported by wiring Code Word "BRUEUS" to this H.Qrs. and verbally by O.C. D. Company to H.Qrs. 127th Inf. Bde.

7. ACKNOWLEDGE.

 Culson Capt. & Adjt.,
 42nd. Battalion, M.G.C.

Distribution.
Copies No. 1 to 4. A.B.C.& D. Coys.
 " " 5. 42nd. Division 'G'
 " " 6. H.Q. 127th Inf. Bde.
 " " 7. IV Corps M.G.Officer.
 " " 8 & 9. War Diary.
 " " 10. File.

Vol. 3

CONFIDENTIAL
ORIGINAL

WAR DIARY.

OF

42ND BATTALION MACHINE GUN CORPS.

(VOLUME 3)

FROM 1-5-18.
TO 31-5-18.

WAR DIARY
or
INTELLIGENCE SUMMARY.
(Erase heading not required.)

Army Form C. 2118.

Place	Date	Hour	Summary of Events and Information	Remarks and references to Appendices
COUIN	1-5-18		Dull, visibility bad. Situation normal. Enemy artillery moderately active, GOMMECOURT PARK very heavily shelled. Our artillery usual activity. Enemy MGs very active during night. Our MGs fired 8,000 rounds harassing fire on usual targets. Work night firing positions improved, new gun emplacements continued, prisoners' positions & shelters improved. Casualties nil.	CRR
	2-5-18		Sun above all day, warm, visibility fair only due to mist rising from ground. Enemy artillery showed increased activity. BIEZ SWITCH, GOMMECOURT WOOD and vicinity shelled throughout the day. E 29 b + d. and E 30 c heavily shelled about 3 P.M. Our artillery was very active throughout the day + night. Our M.Gs fired 7000 rds on trenches L13 b 95 50 and L14 a 2 6 and usual targets. Enemy M.Gs very active between 8 30 P.M - 5 A.M. Considerable aerial activity. Emplacements to emplacements + trenches in vicinity continued, several new emplacements + shelters commenced. Casualties nil.	CRR
	3-5-18		Sunny all day, warm, visibility good. Vicinity of COUIN shelled by H.V. gun during early hours of the morning, all shells fell in open ground. Enemy artillery fairly active. FONQUEVILLERS heavily shelled throughout the day. Enemy MGs fired into GOMMECOURT. Our M.Gs fired 8000 rounds ats usual targets. Enemy and our aircraft very active. Work several new emplacements commenced, improvements to trenches etc continued, shelters constructed + camouflaged. Casualties Wounded 1 O.R.	CRR
	4-5-18		Sun shone all day, warm, visibility good. Enemy artillery active, especially in vicinity of GOMMECOURT. Our artillery very active, a very heavy barrage was put down at 8.50 P.M. in cooperation with operations on our right by N.Z. Division. Our M.Gs fired 4000 rounds on usual targets. Enemy aeroplanes very active. Work on emplacements etc continued. Casualties nil.	CRR

A3834 Wt. W.4973/M687 750,000 8/16 D.D. & L. Ltd. Forms/C.2118/13.

Army Form C. 2118.

WAR DIARY
or
INTELLIGENCE SUMMARY.
(Erase heading not required.)

Place	Date	Hour	Summary of Events and Information	Remarks and references to Appendices
COUIN	5-5-18		Rain in early morning and also later in the day; clear; visibility very low. Artillery, enemy quieter than usual. Gun mists & trench mortar were normal. Enemy M.Gs. showed much activity, particularly over our positions at K.6.a. Hostile aircraft dropped a dozen bombs on our sector. Work. The usual improvements were continued and two emplacements in HERRING TRENCH were completed. Casualties nil.	eeR
	6-5-18		Dull, visibility low, heavy rain at night. Situation on the front quiet. The vicinity of COUIN was shelled by H.V. gun between 1.30 P.M. & 2.30 P.M. Relief of 42nd Battn.M.G.C. by 57th Battn.M.G.C. commenced. 'C' Coy 42nd Battn. M.G.C. moved from J.2.d. 6.3. to bivouacs at D.27.d.6.3. slightly shelled at 10 A.M. Rest camp party returned to their Coys during the course of the day. 'B' Coy 42nd Battn M.G.C. were relieved in the line & proceeded to billets in HENU, relief was completed at 11.20 P.M. Casualties nil.	APP I
	7-5-18		W.e.C. in the morning, fine later, visibility poor. Artillery enemy quieter than usual. 2 Sections of 'D' Coy 42nd Battn.M.G.C. in the line were relieved in the early morning & proceeded to movements near COIGNEUX, 2 Section of 'D' Coy 42nd Battn. M.G.C. in reserve at J.2.d.9.4. relieved two Sections 57th Battn M.G.C. in the CHATEAU de la HAIE SWITCH, relief was completed at 11.25 A.M. Reconnaissance of the RED LINE was commenced. 'A' Coy 42nd Battn. M.G.C. in the line was relieved by 57th Battn M.G.C. & proceeded to billets near COIGNEUX, relief was completed at 9.35 P.M. Casualties nil.	eeR APP II
PAS.	8-5-18		Sunny, nice, visibility good. Battn H.Q. moved to PAS. Move was completed at midday. Coys commenced bathing & refitting.	eeR

Army Form C. 2118.

WAR DIARY
or
INTELLIGENCE SUMMARY.
(Erase heading not required.)

Instructions regarding War Diaries and Intelligence Summaries are contained in F. S. Regs. Part II and the Staff Manual respectively. Title pages will be prepared in manuscript.

Place	Date	Hour	Summary of Events and Information	Remarks and references to Appendices
P.A.S.	8.5.18 (continued)		Reconnaissance of Red Line continued	ccR
	9.5.18	7 AM	Sunny all day; hot; visibility poor early; but improved considerably later. Were relieved from 4.2nd Div entering practice occupation of positions in RED LINE. This was carried out by Coys in accordance with APP II. Coys returned to billets during the course of the day.	ccR
	10.5.18		Full during the early part of the day; sunny later when visibility improved. The day was devoted to M.G. training, P.T. & sports.	ccR
	11.5.18		Dull all day; visibility poor. All Coys carried out the following training; elementary M.G. work, P.T. and sports.	ccR
	12.5.18		Dull all day; slight rain in the morning; visibility poor	ccR
	13.5.18		Rain all day; colder; visibility very bad. All Coys inspected by C.O during the course of the day. The following training was carried out, P.T & B.F. Elementary M.G. Training, Range Drill & mounting. Officers + N.C.O. classes were also commenced	ccR
	14.5.18		Dull, sun shone occasionally; visibility fair. Training carried out in accordance with APP III	APP III ccR
	15.5.18		Sun shone all day, hot; visibility good. Training carried out in accordance with APP IV	APP IV ccR
	16.5.18		Draft of 40 O.R. joined battalion from Base Depot. Very hot; sun shone all day; visibility very good. A, B, + C Coys inspected by IV Corps Commander, after inspection 'A' Coy carried out a tactical exercise.	APP V ccR

Army Form C. 2118.

WAR DIARY or INTELLIGENCE SUMMARY.
(Erase heading not required.)

Instructions regarding War Diaries and Intelligence Summaries are contained in F. S. Regs., Part II and the Staff Manual respectively. Title pages will be prepared in manuscript.

Place	Date	Hour	Summary of Events and Information	Remarks and references to Appendices
PAS	17-5-18		Very hot, sun shone all day, visibility very good.	cf APP VI
	18-5-18		Training carried out in accordance with APP VI. Very hot, sunny, heavy thunderstorm during afternoon, visibility very good. Battalion syjallers practiced communications in accordance with RED LINE Scheme. Training was carried out in accordance with APP VII.	APP VII cf
	19-5-18		Hot, sun shone all day, visibility very good. Vicinity of COIGNEUX shelled at night with H.E. and Gas shells.	cf
	20-5-18		Very hot, sun shone all day, visibility very good. Training was carried out in accordance with APP VIII. Also 1 Off + 240 O.R. per Coy received training in "Lewis Gun"	cf APP VIII
	21-5-18		Very hot, sunny all day, visibility very good. Practice occupation of positions in accordance with RED LINE Scheme. "Battle Position" was sent out from Batt. H.Q. at 3A.M. Coys went in position at the following times "A" Coy at 5.50 A.M; "B" Coy at 5.10 A.M; "C" Coy at 6.48 A.M; "D" Coy at 5.25 A.M. The exercise was carried out in a highly satisfactory manner, and went without a hitch.	cf
	22-5-18		Very hot, sunny all day with the exception of an hour in the afternoon when a thunder storm passed over. Visibility very good. Training was carried out in accordance with APP IX and in addition all officers + N.C.O's instructing and over the rank of Corporal attended a Lecture on "Gas".	APP IX cf
	23-5-18		Dull all day, much cooler, strong wind, rain fell during middle of day. Training was carried out in accordance with APP X. A draft of 30 O.R. joined from Base Depot.	cf APP X
	24-5-18		Gloomy grey all day, visibility bad, much colour	

WAR DIARY or INTELLIGENCE SUMMARY

Army Form C. 2118.

Place	Date	Hour	Summary of Events and Information	Remarks and references to Appendices
PAS	24-5-18		Training carried out in accordance with APP XI	APP XI
			100 officers & O.Rs. of the Battalion, were fitted with new respirators & passed through the gas chamber	c/R
			Sunny, hot, visibility good.	
	25-5-18		Training carried out in accordance with APP XII. Signalling personnel carried out a practice occupation of RED LINE positions, all practice messages were transmitted satisfactorily	APP XII
			A further 260 officers & O.Rs. were fitted with new respirators & their respirators + their resp.[?] through the gas	c/R
			A draft of 6 O.R joined from Base Depot	
			Sun all day, own shower at intervals, visibility good.	
	26-5-18		A further 260 O.R were fitted with new respirators etc	c/R
			Fine, sunny in the morning, cloudy later, visibility good	
	27-5-18		Training carried out in accordance with APP XIII. All available officers & O.R.'s completed with new respirators & G.S.B.R etc	APP XIII c/R
			Sun shower all day, not, visibility good	
	28-5-18		Training carried out in accordance with APP XIV	APP XIV c/R
			Sun all day, cloudy early, sun shown at intervals, visibility good	
	29-5-18		Training carried out in accordance with APP XV	APP XV c/R
			Sunny all day, visibility excellent	
	30-5-18		Training carried out in accordance with APP XVI.	APP XVI c/R
			Presentation of ribbons was carried out by G.O.C. during the course of the morning in the vicinity of COUIN	
			COIGNEUX and vicinity, suffered casualties. Killed: 1 O.R.	

Army Form C. 2118.

WAR DIARY
or
INTELLIGENCE SUMMARY.

(Erase heading not required.)

Place	Date	Hour	Summary of Events and Information	Remarks and references to Appendices
PAS	31-5-18		Wet, sunny at day, visibility very good. 2 Officers joined Battn from M.G.C Base Depot. Training was carried out in accordance with APP XVII	APP XVIII cef

N. K. Tebbits
Lieut Col.
Comg 42nd Battn M.G.C.

SECRET.   APP I   Copy No. 8

42nd. Battalion, M.G.C. Order No. 15.

May 3rd. 1918.

1. The 42nd. Battalion, M.G.C. will be relieved in the line by the 57th Battalion, M.G.C. on the nights 6/7th. and 7/8th. May.

2. The Right Group of 24 Guns consisting of 16 Guns B. Company and 8 Guns D. Company will be relieved on the night 6/7th.

3. The Left Group of 16 Guns of A. Company will be relieved on night 7/8th.

4. All details of relief will be arranged between O's. C. M.G. Companies concerned.

5. On relief of Right Group (6/7th. May) B. Company will move to HENU and take over billets vacated by D. Company, 57th. Battalion, M.G.C. D. Company, less 8 guns will move into huts in Camp South of COIGNEUX J.9.d.Central, vacated by C. Company, 57th. Bn. M.G.C.

6. One relief Left Group (A. Company, 7/8th. May) will move into huts in Camp South of COIGNEUX, J.9.d.Central vacated by B. Company, 57th. Bn. M.G.C.

7. On the 7th. May, C. Company will move into Camp at D.27.d.6.3.

8. On the morning of the 7th. before 9.30a.m. 8 guns of D. Company will relieve 8 guns of the 57th. Battalion, M.G.C. in the CHATEAU de la HAIE Switch - Company Headquarters J.5.d.7.2.

9. Trench Maps, Range Cards, Local Defence Schemes etc. will be handed over.

10. The Regimental Sergeant Major will have an accurate statement showing the location and size of S.A.A. Dumps ready to hand over.

11. Battalion Headquarters will open at Camp. S. of COIGNEUX at 10.30a.m. on the 8th instant.

12. All Battle Surplus will be withdrawn from Billets in COUIN immediately Companies leave the trenches.

13. Relief Complete to be reported by using Code Word "RIFLE".

14. ACKNOWLEDGE.

Distribution.
Copies 1 to 4. A.B.C.& D.Coys.
" No. 5. 42nd. Division 'G'
" " 6. IV Corps M.G.Officer.
" " 7. O.C. 57th. Bn. M.G.C.
" " 8 & 9. War Diary.
" " 10. File.
" " 11. T.O. 42nd. Battalion, M.G.C.
" " 12. Q.M.   - do -
" " 13. R.S.M. - do -

C C Rose
Capt & Adj
for Lieut-Colonel,
Cmdg. 42nd. Battalion, M.G.C.

War Diary

```
O.C.  A.Coy          42nd. Divn. "A".
      B.Coy.           "      "    "Q".
      C.Coy.         O.M.G.O.
      D.Coy.         Batt. Transport Offr.
```

The following changes in location as previously indicated will take place:-

```
    Batt. H.Q.             PAS.
R   Q.M. Stores)
    Refilling Point)       HENU
    A.Coy.                 COIGNEUX Huts I.9.c.
    B.Coy.                 HENU.
    C.Coy.                 D.27.d.C.2.
    D.Coy.                 COIGNEUX Huts I.9.c.
```

                                                  ccRoss Capt. & Adjt.
7/5/19.   42nd. Batt., M.G.C.

APP III

TRAINING PROGRAMME for Tuesday, May 14th. 1918.

'A' and 2 Sections 'D' Coy.

      9a.m. – 10a.m.   P.T. & B.F.

      10.15a.m.   Company Parade and Inspection by O.C. Coy.

      10.20a.m. – 11a.m. Squad Drill – Handling of Arms – Saluting by numbers.

      11.15a.m. – 1p.m.   Section Schemes (which in the course of 4 days training will bring out all the undermentioned points).

(a). Sections advancing with Scouts put out.
(b). Sections coming into action from packs.
(c). Sections coming into action from limbers.
(d). Paralleling Guns; Fighting Maps.
(e). Digging of slit emplacements as used in last Sector of line held.
(f). Visual communication and sending of messages.
(g). Wearing of Respirators during parts of schemes.

      5.30p.m. – 6.30p.m. Officers and N.C.Os' Class under Major R.A.Helps, and R.S.M.

    Section schemes must be reconnoitred by O.C. Companies and Section Officers.   A short lecture to all ranks participating will be given on the previous evening so as to refresh the minds of all on the various points of training being brought out on the ensuing day.

    Attention of O.Cs. Coys. is particularly directed to S.S.152 Appendix xxii 'A' – 'B' and 'C'

                       (signed) C.C.Rose, Capt. & Adjt.,
                               42nd. Battalion, M.G.C.

13/5/18.

App III

TRAINING PROGRAMME for Tuesday, May 14th, 1918.

B. Company.

    8a.m. —   Company Parade and Inspection by O.C. Coy.

    8.5a.m. — 9.50a.m. Squad Drill — Handling of Arms —
                          Saluting by numbers.

    10.15am. — 11.45a.m. Section Schemes (which in the course of
                          4 days training will bring out the
                          undermentioned points.

(a). Sections advancing with Scouts put out.
(b). Sections coming into action from packs.
(c). Sections coming into action from limbers.
(d). Paralleling Guns; Fighting Maps.
(e). Digging of slit emplacements as used in last Sector of line held.
(f). Visual communication and sending of messages.
(g). Wearing of Respirators during parts of scheme.

    12 Noon — 1p.m.   P.T. & B.F.

    Section Schemes must be reconnoitred by O.C. Company and Section Officers.
    A short lecture to all ranks participating will be given on the previous evening so as to refresh the minds of all on the various points of training brought out on the ensuing day.
    Attention of O.C. Company is particularly directed to S.S.152 Appendix xxii 'A' & 'B' and 'C'.

                          (signed) C.G. Rose, Capt. & Adjt.,
                                42nd. Battalion, M.G.C.

13/5/18.

App III

TRAINING PROGRAMME for MAY, 14th 1918.

C. Company. 8.45am – 10.15am. Section Schemes (which in the course of 4 days training will bring out all the undermentioned points.

(a) Sections advancing with Scouts put out.
(b) Sections coming into action from packs.
(c) Sections coming into action from limbers.
(d) Paralleling guns; Fighting Maps.
(e) Digging of slit emplacements as used in last Sector of line held.
(f) Visual communication and sending of messages.
(g) Wearing of Respirators during part of Schemes.

10.30a.m. – 11.30a.m. P.T. & B.F.

11.45a.m. Company Parade and Inspection by O.C. Coy.

11.50a.m. – 12.45p.m. Squad Drill – Handling of Arms – Saluting by numbers.

5.30p.m. – 6.30p.m. Officers and N.C.Os. Class under Major R.A.Helps and R.S.M.

Section Schemes must be reconnoitred by O.C. Company and Section Officers.

A short lecture to all ranks participating will be given on the previous evening so as to refresh the minds of all on the various points of training being brought out on the ensuing day.

Attention of O.C. Company is particularly directed to S.S.152 Appendix. xxii 'A' – 'B' → and 'C'

(signed) C.C.Rose, Capt. & Adjt.,
42nd. Battalion, M.G.C.

13/5/18.

42nd. BATTALION, MACHINE GUN CORPS.
TRAINING PROGRAMME FOR WEDNESDAY, MAY 15th. 1918.

APP IV

"A" Company. & 2 Sections 'D' Coy.	"B" Company.	"C" Company.
9a.m. – 10a.m. P.T. & B.F.	9a.m. – 10a.m. Coy. Parade. Inspection by O.C.Coy. Squad Drill. Handling of Arms. Saluting by numbers.	8.45a.m. – 10.15a.m. Section Schemes.
10.15a.m. – 11a.m. Coy. Parade. Inspection by O.C.Coy. Squad Drill. Handling of Arms. Saluting by numbers.	10.15a.m. – 11.45a.m. Section Schemes.	10.30a.m. – 11.30a.m. P.T. & B.F.
11.15a.m. – 1p.m. Section Schemes.	12 noon – 1p.m. P.T. & B.F.	11.45a.m. – 12.45p.m. Coy. Parade. Inspection by O.C.Coy. Squad Drill. Handling of Arms. Saluting by numbers.
2.15p.m. – 3p.m. Musketry & Revolver Training.	2.15p.m. – 3p.m. Musketry & Revolver Training.	2.15p.m. – 3p.m. Musketry & Revolver Training.
5.30p.m. – 6.30p.m. Officers & N.C.Os. Class.		5.30p.m. – 6.30p.m. Officers & N.C.Os. Class.

May 14th. 1918.

(signed) C.C. Rose, Capt. & Adjt.,
42nd. Battalion, M.G.C.

APP V

42nd. BATTALION, MACHINE GUN CORPS.
TRAINING PROGRAMME FOR THURSDAY, MAY 16th. 1918.

"A" Company.	"B" Company.	"C" Company.
Morning.	Morning.	Morning.
Inspection by Corps Commander.	Inspection by Corps Commander.	Inspection by Corps Commander.
Afternoon.	Afternoon.	Afternoon.
Games.	Games.	Games.
5.30p.m. - 6.30p.m.	5.30p.m. - 6.30p.m.	5.30p.m. - 6.30p.m.
Officers & N.C.Os. Class.	Officers & N.C.Os. Class.	Officers & N.C.Os. Class.

May 15th. 1918.

(signed) C.C.Rose, Capt. & Adjt.,
42nd. Battalion, M.G.C.

42nd. BATTALION, MACHINE GUN CORPS.
TRAINING PROGRAMME FOR FRIDAY, MAY 17th. 1918.

"A" Company.	"B" Company.	"C" Company.
9a.m. – 10a.m. P.T. & B.F.	9a.m. – 10a.m. Coy. Parade. Inspection by O.C.Coy. Squad Drill. Handling of Arms. Saluting by numbers.	8.45a.m. – 10.15a.m. Section Schemes.
10.15a.m. – 11a.m. Coy. Parade. Inspection by O.C.Coy. Squad Drill. Handling of Arms. Saluting by numbers.	10.15a.m. – 11.45a.m. Section Schemes.	10.30a.m. – 11.30a.m. P.T. & B.F.
11.15a.m. – 1p.m. Section Schemes.	12 noon – 1p.m. P.T. & B.F.	11.45a.m. – 12.45p.m. Coy. Parade. Inspection by O.C.Coy. Squad Drill. Handling of Arms. Saluting by numbers.
2.15p.m. – 3p.m. Musketry & Revolver Training.	2.15p.m. – 3p.m. Musketry & Revolver Training.	2.15p.m. – 3p.m. Musketry & Revolver Training.
5.30p.m. – 6.30p.m. Officers & N.C.Os. Class.		5.30p.m. – 6.30p.m. Officers & N.C.Os. Class.

May 16th. 1918.

(signed) C.C.Rose, Capt. & Adjt.,
42nd. Battalion, M.G.C.

App VII

42nd. BATTALION, MACHINE GUN CORPS.
TRAINING PROGRAMME FOR SATURDAY, MAY 18th. 1918.

'A' Company.

9a.m. - 10a.m.
P.T. & B.F.

10.15a.m. - 11a.m.
Coy. Parade.
Inspection by O.C.Coy.
Squad Drill.
Handling of Arms.
Saluting by numbers.

11.15a.m. - 1p.m.
Section Schemes.

Afternoon.
Games.

5.30p.m. - 6.30p.m.
Officers & N.C.Os. Class.

May 17th. 1918.

'B' Company.

9a.m. - 10a.m.
Coy. Parade.
Inspection by O.C.Coy.
Squad Drill.
Handling of Arms.
Saluting by numbers.

10.15a.m. - 11.45a.m.
Section Schemes.

12 noon - 1p.m.
P.T. & B.F.

Afternoon.
Games.

'C' Company.

8.45a.m. - 10.15a.m.
Section Schemes.

10.30a.m. - 11.30a.m.
P.T. & B.F.

11.45a.m. - 12.45p.m.
Coy. Parade.
Inspection by O.C.Coy.
Squad Drill.
Handling of Arms.
Saluting by numbers.

Afternoon.
Games.

5.30p.m. - 6.30p.m.
Officers & N.C.Os.Class.

(signed) C.C.Rose, Capt. & Adjt.
42nd. Battalion, M.G.C.

War Diary

APP VIII

42nd. BATTALION, MACHINE GUN CORPS.
TRAINING PROGRAMME FOR MONDAY, MAY 20th 1918.

A. Company & Two Sections D. Coy.	B. Company.	C. Company.
9a.m. – 10a.m. P.T. & B.F.	9a.m. – 10a.m. Coy. Parade. Inspection by O.C.Coy. Squad Drill. Handling of Arms. Saluting by numbers.	9.45a.m. – 10.15a.m. Section Schemes.
10.15a.m. – 11a.m. Coy. Parade. Inspection by O.C.Coy. Squad Drill. Handling of Arms. Saluting by numbers.	10.15a.m. – 11.45a.m. Section Schemes.	10.30a.m. – 11.30a.m. P.T. & B.F. 11.45a.m. – 12.45p.m. Coy. Parade. Inspection by O.C.Coy. Squad Drill. Handling of Arms. Saluting by numbers.
11.15a.m. – 1p.m. Section Schemes.	12 noon – 1p.m. P.T. & B.F.	
2.15p.m. – 3p.m. Musketry & Revolver Training.	2.15p.m. – 3p.m. Musketry & Revolver Training.	2.15p.m. – 3p.m. Musketry & Revolver Training.
5.30p.m. – 6.30p.m. Officers & N.C.Os. Class.		5.30p.m. – 6.30p.m. Officers & N.C.Os. Class.

May 19th. 1918.

(signed) C.C.Rose, Capt. & Adjt.,
42nd. Battalion, M.G.C.

APP IX

42nd. BATTALION, MACHINE GUN CORPS.
TRAINING PROGRAMME FOR WEDNESDAY, MAY 22nd. 1918.

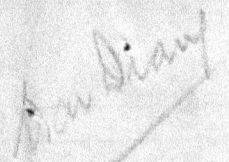

'A' Company & 2 Sections 'D' Coy.	'B' Company.	'C' Company.
8.45a.m. – 9.45a.m. P.T. & B.F.	9a.m. – 10a.m. Squad Drill. Handling of Arms. Saluting by numbers.	9a.m. – 10a.m. Squad Drill. Handling of Arms. Saluting by numbers.
10a.m. – 10.45a.m. Squad Drill. Handling of Arms. Saluting by numbers.	10.30a.m. – 11.45a.m. Section Schemes.	10.15a.m. – 11.15a.m. P.T. & B.F.
11.a.m. – 12.45p.m. Section Schemes.	12 noon – 1p.m. P.T. & B.F.	11.30a.m. – 1p.m. Section Schemes.
5.30p.m. – 6.30p.m. Officers & N.C.Os. Class.		5.30p.m. – 6.30p.m. Officers & N.C.Os. Class.

May 20th. 1918.

(signed) C.C. Rose, Capt. & Adjt.,
42nd. Battalion, M.G.C.

APP X

42nd. BATTALION, MACHINE GUN CORPS.

TRAINING PROGRAMME FOR THURSDAY, MAY 23rd, 1918.

'A' Company & 2 Sections 'D' Company.	'B' Company.	'C' Company.
9.a.m. – 10a.m. P.T. & B.F.	9a.m. – 10a.m. Coy. Parade. Inspection by O.C.Coy. Squad Drill. Handling of Arms. Saluting by numbers.	8.45a.m. – 10.15a.m. Section Schemes.
10.15a.m. – 11a.m. Coy. Parade. Inspection by O.C.Coy. Squad Drill. Handling of Arms. Saluting by numbers.	10.15a.m. – 11.45a.m. Section Schemes.	10.30a.m. – 11.30a.m. P.T. & B.F.
11.15a.m. – 12.m. Section Schemes.	12 noon – 1p.m. P.T. & B.F.	11.45a.m. – 12.45pm Coy. Parade. Inspection by O.C.Coy. Squad Drill. Handling of Arms. Saluting by numbers.
2.15p.m. – 3p.m. Musketry & Revolver Training.	2.15p.m. – 3p.m. Musketry & Revolver Training.	2.15p.m. – 3p.m. Musketry & Revolver Training.
5.30p.m. – 6.30p.m. Officers & N.C.Os. Class.	5.30p.m. – 6.30p.m. Officers & N.C.Os. Class.	5.30p.m. – 6.30p.m. Officers & N.C.Os. Class.

May 21st, 1918.

(signed) O.G.Rose, Capt. & Adjt.;
42nd. Battalion, M.G.C.

APP XI

42nd. BATTALION, MACHINE GUN CORPS.
TRAINING PROGRAMME FOR FRIDAY, MAY 24th. 1918.

'A' Company &
2 Sections 'D' Company.   'B' Company.   'C' Company.

9a.m. - 10a.m.   9a.m. - 10a.m.   8.45a.m. - 10.15a.m.
P.T. & B.F.   Coy. Parade.   Section Schemes.
                                Inspection by O.C.Coy.
                                Squad Drill.   10.30a.m. - 11.30a.m.
                                Handling of Arms.   P.T. & B.F.
                                Saluting by numbers.

10.15a.m. - 11a.m.   10.15a.m. - 11.45a.m.   11.45a.m. - 12.45p.m.
Coy. Parade.   Section Schemes.   Coy. Parade.
Inspection by O.C. Coy.   Inspection by O.C. Coy.
Squad Drill.   Squad Drill.
Handling of Arms.   12 noon - 1p.m.   Handling of Arms.
Saluting by numbers.   P.T. & B.F.   Saluting by numbers.

11.15a.m. - 1p.m.
Section Schemes.

Afternoon.   Afternoon.   Afternoon.
Games.   Games.   Games.

5.30p.m. - 6.30p.m.   5.30p.m. - 6.30p.m.
Officers & N.C.Os. Class.   Officers & N.C.Os. Class.

May 22nd. 1918.   (signed) G.C. Rose, Capt. & Adjt.;
                                                             42nd. Battalion, M.G.C.

42nd. BATTALION, MACHINE GUN CORPS.
TRAINING PROGRAMME FOR SATURDAY, MAY 25th. 1918.

APP XII

'A' Company & 2 Sections 'D' Company.	'B' Company.	'C' Company.
9a.m. – 10a.m. P.T. & B.F.	9a.m. – 10a.m. Coy. Parade. Inspection by O.C.Coy. Squad Drill. Handling of Arms. Saluting by numbers.	8.45a.m. – 10.15a.m. Section Schemes.
10.15a.m. – 11a.m. Coy. Parade. Inspection by O.C.Coy. Squad Drill. Handling of Arms. Saluting by numbers.	10.15a.m. – 11.45a.m. Section Schemes.	10.30a.m. – 11.30a.m. P.T. & B.F.
11.15a.m. – 1p.m. Section Schemes.	12 noon – 1p.m. P.T. & B.F.	11.45a.m. – 12.45p.m. Coy. Parade. Inspection by O.C.Coy. Squad Drill. Handling of Arms. Saluting by numbers.
5.30p.m. – 6.30p.m. Officers & N.C.Os. Class.		5.30p.m. – 6.30p.m. Officers & N.C.Os. Class.

May 23rd. 1918.

(signed) C.C.Rose, Capt. & Adjt.,
 42nd. Battalion, M.G.C.

42nd. BATTALION, MACHINE GUN CORPS.
TRAINING PROGRAMME FOR MONDAY, MAY 27th. 1918.

APP XIII

'A' Company & 2 Sections 'D' Company.	'B' Company.	'C' Company.
9a.m. – 10a.m. P.T. & B.F.	9a.m. – 10a.m. Coy. Parade. Inspection by O.C.Coy. Squad Drill. Handling of Arms. Saluting.	8.45a.m. – 10.15a.m. Section Schemes.
10.15a.m. – 11a.m. Coy. Parade. Inspection by O.C.Coy. Squad Drill. Handling of Arms. Saluting.		10.30a.m. – 11.30a.m. P.T. & B.F.
	10.15a.m. – 11.45a.m. Section Schemes.	11.45a.m. – 12.45p.m. Coy. Parade. Inspection by O.C.Coy. Squad Drill. Handling of Arms. Saluting.
11.15a.m. – 1p.m. Section Schemes.	12 noon – 1p.m. P.T. & B.F.	
2.15p.m. – 5p.m. Barrage Drill.	2.15p.m. – 5p.m. Barrage Drill.	2.15p.m. – 5p.m. Barrage Drill.
5.30p.m. – 6.30p.m. Officers & N.C.Os. Class.		5.30p.m. – 6.30p.m. Officers & N.C.Os. Class.

May 25th. 1918.

(signed) C.C.Rose, Capt. & Adjt.,
42nd. Battalion, M.G.C.

APP XV

42nd. BATTALION, MACHINE GUN CORPS.
TRAINING PROGRAMME FOR WEDNESDAY, MAY 29th. 1918.

'A' Company & 2 Sections 'D' Company.	'B' Company.	'C' Company.
9a.m. - 10a.m. P.T. & B.F. 10.15a.m. - 11a.m. Coy. Parade. Inspection by O.C.Coy. Squad Drill. Handling of Arms. Saluting. 11.15a.m. - 1p.m. Section Schemes. Afternoon. Games. 5.30p.m. - 6.30p.m. Junior N.C.Os. Class.	9a.m. - 10a.m. Coy. Parade. Inspection by O.C.Coy. Squad Drill. Handling of Arms. Saluting. 10.15a.m. - 11.45a.m. Section Schemes. 12 noon - 1p.m. P.T. & B.F. Afternoon. Games.	8.45a.m. - 10.15a.m. Section Schemes. 10.30a.m. - 11.30a.m. P.T. & B.F. 11.45a.m. - 12.45p.m. Coy. Parade. Inspection by O.C.Coy. Squad Drill. Handling of Arms. Saluting. Afternoon. Games. 5.30p.m. - 6.30p.m. Junior N.C.Os. Class.

May 27th. 1918.

(signed) C.C.Rose, Capt. & Adjt.,
42nd. Battalion, M.G.C.

APP XIV

42nd. BATTALION, MACHINE GUN CORPS.
TRAINING PROGRAMME FOR TUESDAY, MAY 28th. 1918.

'A' Company & 2 Sections 'D' Company.	'B' Company.	'C' Company.
9a.m. - 10a.m. P.T. & B.F.	9a.m. - 10a.m. Coy. Parade. Inspection by O.C.Coy. Squad Drill. Handling of Arms. Saluting.	8.45a.m. - 10.15a.m. Section Schemes.
10.15a.m. - 11a.m. Coy. Parade. Inspection by O.C.Coy. Squad Drill. Handling of Arms. Saluting.	10.15a.m. - 11.45a.m. Section Schemes.	10.30a.m. - 11.30a.m. P.T. & B.F.
11.15a.m. - 1p.m. Section Schemes.	12 noon - 1p.m. P.T. & B.F.	11.45a.m. - 12.45p.m. Coy. Parade. Inspection by O.C.Coy. Squad Drill. Handling of Arms. Saluting.
2.15p.m. - 3p.m. Musketry & Revolver Training.	2.15p.m. - 3p.m. Musketry & Revolver Training.	2.15p.m. - 3p.m. Musketry & Revolver Training.
5.30p.m. - 6.30p.m. Officers & N.C.Os. Class.		5.30p.m. - 6.30p.m. Officers & N.C.Os. Class.

May 26th. 1918.

(signed) O.C.Rose, Capt. & Adjt.,
42nd. Battalion, M.G.C.

APP XVI

42nd. BATTALION, MACHINE GUN CORPS.
TRAINING PROGRAMME FOR THURSDAY, MAY 30th. 1918.

'A' Company & 2 Sections 'D' Company.	'B' Company.	'C' Company.
<u>9a.m. - 10a.m.</u> P.T. & B.F.	<u>9a.m. - 10a.m.</u> Coy. Parade. Inspection by O.C.Coy. Squad Drill. Handling of Arms. Saluting.	<u>8.45a.m. - 10.15a.m.</u> Section Schemes.
<u>10.15a.m. - 11a.m.</u> Coy. Parade. Inspection by O.C.Coy. Squad Drill. Handling of Arms. Saluting.		<u>10.30a.m. - 11.30a.m.</u> P.T. & B.F.
	<u>10.15a.m. - 11.45a.m.</u> Section Schemes.	<u>11.45a.m. - 12.45p.m.</u> Coy. Parade. Inspection by O.C.Coy. Squad Drill. Handling of Arms. Saluting.
<u>11.15a.m. - 1p.m.</u> Section Schemes.	<u>12 noon - 1p.m.</u> P.T. & B.F.	
<u>2.15p.m. - 3p.m.</u> Barrage Drill.	<u>2.15p.m. - 3p.m.</u> Barrage Drill.	<u>2.15p.m. - 3p.m.</u> Barrage Drill.
<u>5.30p.m. - 6.30p.m.</u> Junior N.C.Os. Class.		<u>5.30p.m. - 6.30p.m.</u> Junior N.C.Os. Class.

May 29th. 1918.

(signed) C.C.Rose, Capt. & Adjt.,
42nd. Battalion, M.G.C.

App XVII

42nd. BATTALION, MACHINE GUN CORPS.
TRAINING PROGRAMME FOR FRIDAY, MAY 31st. 1918.

'A' Company & 2 Sections 'D' Company.	'B' Company.	'C' Company.
9a.m. - 10a.m. P.T. & B.F.	9a.m. - 10a.m. Coy. Parade. Inspection by O.C.Coy. Squad Drill. Handling of Arms. Saluting.	8.45a.m. - 10.15a.m. Section Schemes.
10.15a.m. - 11a.m. Coy. Parade. Inspection by O.C.Coy. Squad Drill. Handling of Arms. Saluting.	10.15a.m. - 11.45a.m. Section Schemes.	10.30a.m. - 11.30a.m. P.T. & B.F.
11.15a.m. - 1p.m. Section Schemes.	12 noon - 1p.m. P.T. & B.F.	11.45a.m. - 12.45p.m. Coy. Parade. Inspection by O.C.Coy. Squad Drill. Handling of Arms. Saluting.
2.15p.m. - 3p.m. Musketry & Revolver Training.	2.15p.m. - 3p.m. Musketry & Revolver Training.	2.15p.m. - 3p.m. Musketry & Revolver Training.
5.30p.m. - 6.30p.m. Junior N.C.Os. Class.		5.30p.m. - 6.30p.m. Junior N.C.Os. Class.

May 29th. 1918.

(Signed) C.C.Rose, Capt. & Adjt.,
42nd. Battalion, M.G.C.

Vol. IV

CONFIDENTIAL.

WAR DIARY.

OF

42nd BATTALION MACHINE GUN CORPS.

(VOLUME IV)

From 1-6-18.

To 30-6-18.

Army Form C. 2118.

WAR DIARY
or
INTELLIGENCE SUMMARY.
(Erase heading not required.)

Instructions regarding War Diaries and Intelligence Summaries are contained in F. S. Regs., Part II. and the Staff Manual respectively. Title pages will be prepared in manuscript.

Place	Date	Hour	Summary of Events and Information	Remarks and references to Appendices
PAS	1-6-18		Sun shone all day, hot, visibility very good	APP I ccR
	2-6-18		Training was carried out in accordance with APP I. Sunny all day, warm, visibility good. Casualties killed 1.O.R.	ccR
	3-6-18		Sunny all day, visibility very good. Training was carried out in accordance with APP II. Reconnaissance of right sector IV Corps front, at present held by N.Z. Div., commenced, in view of the relief of the N.Z. Div. by the 42nd Div. on the nights 6/7 and 7/8 June.	APP II ccR
	4-6-18		Dull and overcast all day, cooler, visibility fair. Training was carried out in accordance with APP III. Reconnaissance of right sector IV Corps front was continued.	APP III ccR
	5-6-18		Sunny, visibility good. Reconnaissance of front to be taken over was continued. D. Coy relieved 1 Section of A. Coy and 1 Section of C. Coy in the CHATEAU-de-la-HAIE Switch and RED LINE. Relief was completed at 6.30 a.m. Training was carried out in accordance with APP V.	APP IV APP V ccR
	6-6-18		Sun shone all day, hot, visibility good. "B" Coy 42nd Battn M.G.C. relieved AUCKLAND Coy N.Z M.G Battn in the Right Subsector. Coy HQ established at K.25.d. 92.10. Relief was completed at 4.30 p.m.	ccR
BUS	7-6-18		Sunny all day, visibility good; slight shower of rain during night Batt HQ moved to BUS during the course of the afternoon. A. Coy 42nd Battn M.G.C. relieved CANTERBURY Coy N.Z. M.G. Battn in the left support, & left PURPLE LINE	

Army Form C. 2118.

WAR DIARY
or
INTELLIGENCE SUMMARY.
(Erase heading not required.)

Instructions regarding War Diaries and Intelligence Summaries are contained in F.S. Regs., Part II. and the Staff Manual respectively. Title pages will be prepared in manuscript.

Place	Date	Hour	Summary of Events and Information	Remarks and references to Appendices
BUS	7-6-18	(cont)	Coy H Q were established at T.18.d.30.10. Relief was completed at 5.50 p.m.	
			"B" Coy, 42nd Battn M.G.C. was relieved in the CHATEAU-DE-LA-HAIE switch by the OTAGO Coy N.Z. M.G. Battn during the afternoon. Relief was completed at 5 p.m. D Coy 42nd Battn H.G.C. then moved to T.26.b.55. Situation moderately quiet. 6000 rounds harassing fire were expended during the night into selected targets. Work. Reliefs were continued. moderate gun positions + S.A.A. shelters were constructed, and positions improved generally. Casualties nil. Battn Surgeon proceeded to HALLOY.	CCR
			"C" Coy 42nd Battn M.G.C. relieved WELLINGTON Coy. N.Z. H.G. Battn in the left sub sector during the night 7/8 June. Coy H.Q. were established at K.8.d. 95.95. Relief was completed at 6.30 a.m. 7-6-18.	
	8-6-18		Sunny all day. Visibility very good.	
			D Coy 42nd Battn M.G.C. relieved CANTERBURY Coy N.Z.M.G. Battn in the right support & night PURPLE LINE. Relief was completed at 11.45 a.m. Coy H.Q. were established at T.29.a.47.	
			Enemy artillery shelled HEBUTERNE and ridge E. of SAILLY-FONQUEVILLERS Road. M.G. enemy fired several bursts over our position at Q.4.d.9.9. Our M.G's fired 5000 rounds into allotted targets during the night, in conjunction with operation by 17th Division on our immediate right. Our M.G. assisted with the two Vickers 2 guns of B Coy and 6 guns of the 114th Country Squadron M.G.C. (which unit is attached for tactical handling) 15000 rounds were fired by B Coy and 32,000 by the 114th Squadron. Work. Several sites were dug, existing positions were improved. camouflaged and revetted. S.A.A. shelters were constructed. Casualties nil.	CCR
	9-6-18		Fine all day. Dull & overcast. Sun shone at intervals. Light rain in early morning. Visibility fair. Aerial activity normal.	
			6 officers joined from Base Depot.	
			Enemy artillery moderately active, four were shelled with whizz bangs from 3 am – 4 am. FONQUEVILLERS-SAILLY	

WAR DIARY or INTELLIGENCE SUMMARY

Army Form C. 2118.

Place	Date	Hour	Summary of Events and Information	Remarks and references to Appendices
BUS	9-6-18	(cont)	Roads heavily shelled from 2 p.m - 4 p.m. M.Gs enemy fired burst during the night round our positions J.2.a.9.9. Our M.Gs fired 6,500 rounds harassing fire on selected targets during the course of the night. Work continued on sites and dug outs and several new emplacements were commenced, improvements continued. Casualties wounded at duty 1 O.R.	cer
	10-6-18		Dull, some fog during morning and afternoon, visibility poor. Enemy artillery showed usual activity, enemy M.Gs fire periodically through the night. Our M.Gs fired 11,250 rounds harassing fire onto selected targets. Two enemy planes attempted to fly very low over our lines, but were driven off every time by our M.Gs. Work continued on emplacements, dugouts and S.A.A. shelters etc.	cef
	11-6-18		Draft of 11 O.R. joined from M.G.C. Base Depot. Casualties nil. Overcast, sun shone at intervals, visibility fair. Situation on Divisional front quiet. Enemy M.Gs carried out harassing fire during the night on our positions at Q.2.d.99 and K32.b. Our M.Gs fired 7,500 rounds during the night onto selected targets. Work started on several new emplacements, with an N.C.O. contained, general improvements were carried out. Casualties nil.	cer
	12-6-18		Sun shone all day, hot, visibility good. Enemy artillery showed less activity. Our M.Gs fired 7,500 rounds harassing fire onto selected targets. Casualties nil.	cef
	13-6-18		Work was continued on new emplacements + sites. Sun and sunny all day, visibility good. Draft of 1 Officer and 27 O.R. joined from Base Depot. Enemy artillery showed less activity than usual. Enemy M.G's showed usual activity during the night. Our M.Gs fired 10,200 rounds harassing fire onto selected targets. Work was carried on with new + existing	

A5834 Wt.W4973/M687 750,000 8/16 D. D. & L. Ltd. Forms/C.2118/13

Army Form C. 2118.

WAR DIARY
or
INTELLIGENCE SUMMARY.
(Erase heading not required.)

Instructions regarding War Diaries and Intelligence Summaries are contained in F. S. Regs., Part II. and the Staff Manual respectively. Title pages will be prepared in manuscript.

Place	Date	Hour	Summary of Events and Information	Remarks and references to Appendices
BUS	13-6-18 (cont)		emplacements and staff. Casualties nil.	CCR
	14-6-18		Dull, cooler, visibility poor, rain fell during the night. 1 Off. and 24 O.R. joined from Base Depot. Usual activity was shown by the enemy artillery and M.G. Our M.G. fired 7,500 rounds onto selected targets during the course of the night. Work was continued on new and existing emplacements and dug outs. Casualties nil.	CCR
	15-6-18		Sun shone at intervals, cloudy, cool, visibility moderate during the morning, very good later in the day. Enemy artillery was quiet during the day, more active at night. Our M.G. fired 4,000 rounds harassing fire during the night onto selected targets. "C" Coy fired 4,000 rounds in conjunction with artillery bombardment, which supported a raiding operation in the left sector of the divisional front. Considerable aerial activity took place during the first moon hours. The usual work was carried out. Casualties nil.	CCR
	16-6-18		Sun was shone all day, visibility very good. Enemy artillery showed usual activity. There was considerable aerial activity on both sides particularly in the evening. "A" Coy relieved "C" Coy in the left sector of the divisional front, "C" Coy on relief took over positions vacated by "A" Coy. The relief was completed at 8 p.m. Our M.G. fired 5,500 rounds harassing fire during the night onto selected targets.	APP VI
	17-6-18		Sun and sunny, visibility good, rain fell during evening & night. "D" Coy relieved "B" Coy in the right section of the divisional front, "B" Coy on relief took own positions vacated by	CCR / APP VII

Army Form C. 2118.

WAR DIARY
or
INTELLIGENCE SUMMARY.
(Erase heading not required.)

Instructions regarding War Diaries and Intelligence Summaries are contained in F. S. Regs., Part II. and the Staff Manual respectively. Title pages will be prepared in manuscript.

Place	Date	Hour	Summary of Events and Information	Remarks and references to Appendices
BUS	17-6-16	(contin)	"D" Coy. The relief was completed at 5.30 p.m.	
	18-6-16		MESNIL TERRE and ESCARPMENTS were heavily shelled. Enemy also put down fire shrapnel and H.E. barrage during the evening & night, our guns K.22.b.90.50 to K.20.c.central to K.20.a central. Our M.Gs fired 3,500 rounds harassing fire onto selected targets during the night. Work was continued on dug-outs and new gun positions. The camouflaging of positions was improved. Casualties nil.	cR
	19-6-16		Enemy shelled all day, inflicting sweet heat, commenced massing in the evening and continued at night. Draft of 20 O.Rs sent to 63rd Battalion M.G.C. Normal activity on the front. Our M.G. fired 700 rounds harassing fire onto selected targets. Battn Bombers moved from HALLOY to LOUVEN COURT, where a Machine Gun School was commenced by the second in command. 1 O.R. casualty wounded.	
			Enemy was fell with suddenly, sun shone at intervals later, visibility fair. Our artillery bombarded the enemy's lines from 12 midnight to 12.30 am. Activity normal during the remainder of the day & night. Our MGs fired 5500 rounds on to selected targets. One enemy observation balloon descended in flames in the direction of ALBERT. Work was continued on new dugouts & emplacements. Casualties nil.	K
	20-6-16		Heavy rain fell during the day & night, visibility excellent while fine. Enemy activity normal. MAILLY-MAILLET was shelled during the afternoon. Our artillery fire normal. Our MGs fired 5500 rounds on to selected targets during the night. Work on dugouts & emplacements continued. Casualties nil.	K
	21.6.16		Rain fell at intervals during the morning, visibility fair. Artillery activity normal.	

WAR DIARY or INTELLIGENCE SUMMARY

Army Form C. 2118.

(Erase heading not required.)

Instructions regarding War Diaries and Intelligence Summaries are contained in F.S. Regs., Part II. and the Staff Manual respectively. Title pages will be prepared in manuscript.

Place	Date	Hour	Summary of Events and Information	Remarks and references to Appendices
BUS	21.6.18 (cont)		Our M.G. fired 6,000 rounds during the night on to K.28.B.4.9 and K.28.B.0.6. The M.G. barrage was not altered to fit in with the new artillery barrage at 10.0 a.m. These two Bdys have previously fired at 5.0 am and found quite satisfactory. The usual work on dugouts + emplacements was carried out. Casualties nil.	[sgd]
	22.6.18		Fine rain fell during the morning, visibility poor, improved during the afternoon. Enemy artillery active, COLINCAMPS and MAILLY-MAILLET were shelled with heavy H.E. during the day. Our artillery normal, our M.G's fired 6,000 rounds on to K.34.d.5.9 and K.28.B.6.0. Work on dugouts + emplacements continued. Two Sections of B Coy. 42nd Bn M.G.C. carried out an intersection relief with the two Sections garrisoning the RIGHT PURPLE LINE positions. Casualties nil.	[sgd]
	23.6.18		Fine during the day with a strong Westerley wind, visibility very good. The night S.O.S. barrage was tested at 10 am and found quite satisfactory. 1500 rounds were fired. Enemy artillery active during the day. COLINCAMPS and COURCELLES shelled with 105 mm. Our artillery active during the night. Our M.G's fired 6,500 rounds on to K.34.d.5.9 and K.28.B.6.0. Work continued on dugouts + emplacements. Casualties nil.	[sgd]
	24.6.18		Cloudy hot fine during the day. Strong Westerley wind. Visibility fair. Enemy artillery very active from 9.30 pm to midnight. MAILLY-MAILLET, SAILLY and the CEMETERY South of COLINCAMPS were heavily shelled. Our fire normal during the day but increased during the night. Our M.G's fired 6,500 rounds on to 65.a.19 and K.28.b.23. For the average was engaged during the morning without effect. Our planes fired enemy balloons to descend. Two Sections less one Sub-section of B Coy 42nd Bn M.G.C. relieved the guns of the 1st Cavalry Squadron SE of COLINCAMPS. Relief complete 3.0 pm. Work on dugouts + emplacements continued. Casualties nil.	[sgd] App VII
	25.6.18		Weather cloudy hot fine. Visibility excellent. 14th Cavalry Squadron left the boys and proceeded to join the 2nd Div. Enemy artillery very active during the day and night. Our M.G's fired 6,000 rounds on to selected targets during the night. Enemy's M.G's were	[sgd]

WAR DIARY
or
INTELLIGENCE SUMMARY.
(Erase heading not required.)

Army Form C. 2118.

Place	Date	Hour	Summary of Events and Information	Remarks and references to Appendices
BUS	25.6.18 (cont)		active during the night. Both on dugouts & emplacements continued. Casualties nil.	No.
	26.6.18		Fine throughout the day. Visibility fair. During the morning enemy artillery was unusually active especially against our lines communications. Our artillery fire normal. Our M.G's fired 1000 rounds during the night. Both continued on dugouts & emplacements. Casualties nil.	No.
	27.6.18		Fine during the day. Visibility very good. Artillery of both sides active. Enemy M.G. very active during the day against our aircraft. Our M.G's fired 1000 rounds during the night. Both on lines continued. Our hunting planes particularly active. Casualties nil.	No.
	28.6.18		Weather very fine. Light Westerly wind. Visibility excellent. Artillery (enemy) active throughout the day. COLINCAMPS, MAILLY-MAILLET & BEAUSART heavily shelled. Our M.G. fired 1000 rounds during the night. One hostile plane was brought down during the day by our aircraft. Both continued on dugouts. We projected gas on to area about LA SIGNY FARM. Casualties 2/Lt ESSEX wounded. shrapnel in chest.	No.
	29.6.18		Weather very fine, visibility fair, improved during the afternoon. Enemy artillery very active against our Batteries. Our M.G. fired 6000 rounds on to K.34.b.3.9 + K.25.d.5.4 during the night. Hostile M.G. very active. Approx 2000 gas shells were thrown into COLIN CAMPS from hours 9.0 pm - 12.0 midnight. Enemy aircraft may active during the night. Both hostile & own camouflaged in the areas around BUS. Both continued on dugouts & emplacements. Casualties nil.	No.
	30.6.18		Fine during the day. Visibility very good. Increased artillery activity by both sides. COLINCAMPS shelled until 10.5 am and 15cm at 11.0 pm. Our M.G. fired 9500 rounds on its areas in rear of Lt SIGNY FARM Enemy aircraft bombed areas around BUS during the night. "D" Coy relieved by "B" Coy less sec guns 4 hy siz guns of C Coy (Battle surpluses at LOUVEN COURT returned.	No. App VIII

M.N. Lieu Lieut Col
Comp MMG Batn. M.G.C.

APP I

42nd. BATTALION, MACHINE GUN CORPS.
TRAINING PROGRAMME FOR SATURDAY, JUNE 1st. 1918.

'A' Company & 2 Sections 'D' Company.	'B' Company.	'C' Company.
9a.m. – 10a.m. P.T. & B.F. 10.15a.m. – 11a.m. Coy. Parade. Inspection by O.C.Coy. Squad Drill. Handling of Arms. Saluting. 11.15a.m. – 1p.m. Section Schemes. 5.30p.m. – 6.30p.m. Junior N.C.Os. Class.	9a.m. – 10a.m. Coy. Parade. Inspection by O.C.Coy. Squad Drill. Handling of Arms. Saluting. 10.15a.m. – 11.45a.m. Section Schemes. 12noon – 1p.m. P.T. & B.F.	8.45a.m. – 10.15a.m. Section Schemes. 10.30a.m. – 11.30a.m. P.T. & B.F. 11.45a.m. – 12.45p.m. Coy. Parade. Inspection by O.C.Coy. Squad Drill. Handling of Arms. Saluting. 5.30p.m. – 6.30p.m. Junior N.C.Os. Class.

May 30th. 1918.

(signed) C.C.Rose, Capt. & Adjt.,
42nd. Battalion, M.G.C.

APP II

42nd. BATTALION, MACHINE GUN CORPS.
TRAINING PROGRAMME FOR MONDAY, JUNE 3rd. 1918.

'A' Company &
2 Sections 'D' Company.

9a.m. - 10a.m.
P.T. & B.F.

10.15a.m. - 11a.m.
Barrage Drill.

11.15a.m. - 1p.m.
Section Schemes.

5.30p.m. - 6.30p.m.
Junior N.C.Os. Class.

'B' Company.

9a.m. - 10a.m.
Barrage Drill.

10.15a.m. - 11.45a.m.
Section Schemes.

12 noon - 1p.m.
P.T. & B.F.

'C' Company.

8.45a.m. - 10.15a.m.
Section Schemes.

10.30a.m. - 11.30a.m.
P.T. & B.F.

11.45a.m. - 12.45p.m.
Barrage Drill.

5.30p.m. - 6.30p.m.
Junior N.C.Os. Class.

June 1st. 1918.

(signed) C.C.Rose, Capt. & Adjt.,
42nd. Battalion, M.G.C.

App III

42nd. BATTALION, MACHINE GUN CORPS.

TRAINING PROGRAMME FOR TUESDAY, JUNE 4th. 1918.

'A' Company &
2 Sections 'D' Company.

9a.m. - 10a.m.
P.T. & B.F.

10.15a.m. - 11a.m.
Musketry & Revolver Training.

11.15a.m. - 1p.m.
Section Schemes.

5.30p.m. - 6.30p.m.
Junior N.C.Os. Class.

'B' Company.

9a.m. - 10a.m.
Musketry & Revolver Training.

10.15a.m. - 11.45a.m.
Section Schemes.

12 noon - 1p.m.
P.T. & B.F.

'C' Company.

8.45a.m. - 10.15a.m.
Section Schemes.

10.30a.m. - 11.30a.m.
P.T. & B.F.

11.45a.m. - 12.45p.m.
Musketry & Revolver Training.

5.30p.m. - 6.30p.m.
Junior N.C.Os. Class.

June 2nd. 1918.

(signed) C.C. Rose, Capt. & Adjt.,
42nd. Battalion, M.G.C.

SECRET.   Copy No......6....

APP IV

42nd. Battalion, M.G.C. Order No. 10.

June 2nd. 1918.

1. "D" Company will relieve 1 Section of "C" Company and 1 Section of "A" Company in the CHATEAU-de-la-HAIE Switch and RED LINE on 5th instant.
Relief to be complete by 8a.m.

2. O.C. "D" Company will arrange for the taking over and continuation of work as being carried on at present.

3. Completion of relief will be reported to H.Qrs. 42nd. Battalion, M.G.C. by runner.

4. ACKNOWLEDGE.

W. K. Service

Lieut-Colonel,
Cmdg. 42nd. Battalion, M.G.C.

Distribution.
Copy No. 1. A. Coy.
"   "   2. B. "
"   "   3. C. "
"   "   4. D. "
"   "   5. C.R.E. 42nd. Divn.
"   "   6 & 7. War Diary.
"   "   8. File.
"   "   9 & 10. Spare.

APP V

42nd. BATTALION, MACHINE GUN CORPS.
TRAINING PROGRAMME FOR WEDNESDAY, JUNE 5th. 1918.

'A' Company & 	'B' Company.	'C' Company.
9a.m. - 10a.m. P.T. & B.F.	9a.m. - 10a.m. Barrage Drill.	8.45a.m. - 10.15a.m. Section Schemes.
10.15a.m. - 11a.m. Barrage Drill.	10.15a.m. - 11.45a.m. Section Schemes.	10.30a.m. - 11.30a.m. P.T. & B.F.
11.15a.m. - 1p.m. Section Schemes.	12 noon - 1p.m. P.T. & B.F.	11.45a.m. - 12.45p.m. Barrage Drill.
5.30p.m. - 6.30p.m. Junior N.C.Os. Class.		5.30p.m. - 6.30p.m. Junior N.C.Os. Class.

June 3rd. 1918.

(signed) C.C. Rose, Capt. & Adjt.,
42nd. Battalion, M.G.C.

SECRET.   APP VI   Copy No. 10

42nd. BATTALION, M.G.C. ORDER NO. 18.

June 12th. 1918.

1. (a). 'A' Company will relieve 'C' Company in the Left sector of the Divisional Front on the night 16th/17th. June.
   (b). 'C' Company on relief will take up positions vacated by 'A' Company.

2. (a). 'D' Company will relieve 'B' Company in the Right sector of the Divisional Front on the night 17/18th. June.
   (b). 'B' Company on relief will take up positions vacated by 'D' Company.

3. Details of relief will be arranged between O's. C. Companies concerned.

4. All maps, air photographs, programmes of work, and harassing fire maps will be handed over on relief.

5. Completion of relief will be notified to Battn. H.Qrs. by Code Word "HUSSAR".

6. ACKNOWLEDGE.

                                       C.C.Rose Capt. & Adjt.,
                                       42nd. Battalion, M.G.C.

Distribution.
Copies 1 to 4. A.B.C. & D.Coys.
"   No. 5. 125th Inf. Bde.
"   " 6. 126th. "   "
"   " 7. 127th. "   "
"   " 8. 42nd. Division 'G'.
"   " 9 & 10. War Diary.
"   " 11. File.
"   " 12. S.M.G.O.
"   " 13. 14th. Squadron, M.G.C.

SECRET. APP. VII Copy No. 7

42nd. BATTALION, M.G.C. ORDER NO. 69.

June 23rd. 1918.

1.   'B' Company, 42nd. Battalion, M.G.C. will relieve six guns of 14th. M.G. Cavalry Squadron on Right Flank of Divisional Sector tomorrow, June 24th. 1918.

2.   Relief to be complete by 8p.m. June 24th. 1918.

3.   Details of relief will be arranged between O's. C. Companies concerned.

4.   All maps, air photographs, programmes of work, and harassing fire maps will be handed over on relief.

5.   Completion of relief will be notified to Battalion H.Qrs. by Code Word "BETTER".

6.   ACKNOWLEDGE.

Lieut-Colonel,
Cmdg. 42nd. Battalion, M.G.C.

Distribution.
Copy No. 1. 'B' Coy.
" " 2. 14th. Cavalry Squadron.
" " 3. 42nd. Division 'G'.
" " 4. C.M.G.O. IV Corps.
" " 5. H.Q. 127th. Inf. Bde.
" " 6 & 7. War Diary.
" " 7. File.

SECRET.   App VIII   Copy No. 11

42nd. Battalion, M.G.C. Order No. 20.

June 29th. 1918.

In view of the changing of the Northern Divisional Boundary and Inter-Brigade Boundary, the following reliefs will take place:-

1. On night 30th June/1st. July 'B' Company will relieve 'D' Company less the 6 Northern M.Gs. in the Right Sub-sector. (The approximate map reference of these six guns is - K.19.d. K.20.c. and d.)

2. 'C' Company will relieve 6 Northern guns of 'D' Company (map reference as above).

3. On relief 'D' Company will take over the positions lately vacated by 'B' Company in Right Support (Right PURPLE LINE Area).

4. On the night 1st/2nd July, the N.Z. M.G. Battalion will release 10 M.Gs. of 'A' Company in the Left Sub-sector.

5. 'C' Company will relieve 6 M.Gs. of 'A' Company in Left Sub-sector.(The approximate map reference of these six guns is - K.21.a. K.14.d. K.15.d.)

6. On relief 'A' Company will take over the positions lately vacated by 'C' Company in Left Support (Left PURPLE LINE Area).

7. On July 3rd. 'C' Company will take over 2 M.Gs. from 'A' Company astride track at K.14.c.8.4.

8. On relief 'A' Company will take over from 'D' Company positions for 2 M.Gs. at J.30.b.2.2.

9. The 2 M.Gs. thus released will move into positions to be selected in P.6.b. near CEMETERY.

10. Details of relief will be arranged between O's. C. Companies concerned.

11. Special harassing fire maps, programmes of work in hand and proposed, will be handed over on relief.

12. Completion of relief will be notified to Battalion H.Qrs. by Code Word "PIAVE".

13. ACKNOWLEDGE.

Lieut-Colonel,
Cmdg. 42nd. Battalion, M.G.C.

Distribution.
Copies 1 to 4. A.B.C. & D.Coys.
" No. 5. 42nd. Division 'G'
" " 6. H.Q. 125th Inf. Bde.
" " 7. 126th. " "
" " 8. " 127th. " "
" " 9. N.Z. M.G.Battn.
" " 10. C.M.G.O.
" " 11 & 12. War Diary.
" " 13. File.

CONFIDENTIAL.

ORIGINAL.

WAR DIARY.

OF

42ⁿᵈ BATTALION

MACHINE GUN CORPS

FROM 1-7-18

To 31-7-18

Army Form C. 2118.

WAR DIARY
or
INTELLIGENCE SUMMARY.
(Erase heading not required.)

Instructions regarding War Diaries and Intelligence Summaries are contained in F. S. Regs., Part II. and the Staff Manual respectively. Title pages will be prepared in manuscript.

Place	Date	Hour	Summary of Events and Information	Remarks and references to Appendices
BUS	1-7-18		Sunny all day, hot, visibility good. N.Z Machine Gun Battalion relieved 10 guns of "A" Coy in the Right Subsector. "C" Coy relieved 6 guns of "A" Coy in the Left subsector, "A" Coy on relief took own positions vacated by "C" Coy in Left Support. Relief was completed at 9 P.M.	ccf
	2-7-18		Situation on the front was quiet all day, but after 11 P.M. all arms were very active during the remainder of the night. Vicinity of LOUVENCOURT and BUS was shelled and several bombs were dropped during the night. Our M.Gs fired 19,000 rounds in co-operation with artillery barrage covering raiding parties of the 126th and Brigade, who raided opposite the right sub sector. Work on dugouts and emplacements continued. No casualties. Sun shone all day, visibility very good. "C" Coy Sgt Batten M.G.C moved into billets in BUS and came under the tactical control of 4th Division. Enemy artillery showed rather more activity than usual, particularly at night. Our M.Gs fired 3,750 rounds harassing fire onto selected targets. Enemy M.G's were very active, firing many bursts onto areas K.20.d K32.b+K.20.c. Aerial activity less active than usual, one hostile plane was driven off by our M.G gun. Work continued on dugouts, shelters in K.31.b were improved. Casualties wounded at duty, 1 O.R.	ccf
	3-7-18		Sun shone all day, windy, cooler, visibility good. "C" Coy took over 2 guns from "A" Coy astride track at K.14.c.8.4 and on relief "A" Coy took	

A5834—Wt.W4973/M687 750,000 8/16 D. D. & L. Ltd. Forms/C.2118/13.

Army Form C. 2118.

WAR DIARY
or
INTELLIGENCE SUMMARY.
(Erase heading not required.)

Instructions regarding War Diaries and Intelligence Summaries are contained in F. S. Regs., Part II and the Staff Manual respectively. Title pages will be prepared in manuscript.

Place	Date	Hour	Summary of Events and Information	Remarks and references to Appendices
BUS	3.7.16 (cont)		Our 2 guns from D Coy at 1.30 to 2.2 the 2 guns of D Coy after relief moved into positions in P.6.c near the CEMETRY	
			Enemy artillery showed more activity than usual, our own artillery were especially active at night. Our M.G's fired 4000 rounds harassing fire onto selected targets. Two hostile planes were driven off by own M.G. guns about 8.10 am. Work was continued on dug-outs & new emplacements. The camouflaging of several shifts was completed. Casualties nil	ceR
	4.7.16		Dull & overcast early in the day, sun shone later when visibility improved. 16 guns of "C" Coy 87a Bn. M.G.C. moved up into positions in reserve zones of defence in the following vicinities, 1 Section P.5.a ¼, section J.3.4 & central, 1 section J.3.4 & central, 1 subsection J.17 G.1.1 - 1 sub section J.18.C (QUARRY) Enemy artillery showed considerable activity, particularly at night. Enemy M.G. fire onto K.26.c & d and K.25.b & d during the course of the night. Our M.G's fired 3,500 rounds harassing fire onto selected targets. The usual work was continued. Casualties nil.	ceR
	5.7.16		Dull & overcast, sun shone later, visibility poor. Situation on the front quiet during the day, activity slightly increased during the night. Enemy M.G's displayed usual activity during the night. Our M.G. fired 3,750 rounds harassing fire during the night onto selected targets. An enemy plane flew over our lines at about 10 pm & was driven off by M.G's. Usual work on dug-outs and emplacements was continued. Casualties nil.	ceR

Army Form C. 2118.

WAR DIARY
or
INTELLIGENCE SUMMARY.
(Erase heading not required.)

Instructions regarding War Diaries and Intelligence Summaries are contained in F. S. Regs., Part II. and the Staff Manual respectively. Title pages will be prepared in manuscript.

Place	Date	Hour	Summary of Events and Information	Remarks and references to Appendices
BUS	6-7-18		Overcast, sun shone at intervals when visibility improved, but there was no unusual activity displayed by the enemy. The usual intermittent shelling took place. Our M.Gs fired 3,750 rounds harassing fire onto selected targets during the course of the night. A hostile plane was driven off by our M.G. gun about 11.30 a.m. whilst camouflage work & improvement of site and emplacements continued. Also work on dug-outs. Casualties nil.	S.O.R.
	7-7-18		Very hot, sun shone all day, visibility excellent. Enemy artillery showed more activity than usual, firing onto usual targets. Our own artillery was very active at night. Our M.Gs fired 3,250 rounds harassing fire onto selected targets. An aircraft was very active during the whole 24 hours. Hand work was continued & was kept up round several gun positions. Casualties wounded A.O.R. accidentally wounded 1 O.R.	S.O.R.
	8-7-18		Very hot, sunny in the morning, overcast later, visibility good; rain fell during the night. Enemy artillery showed less activity than usual. Enemy M.Gs fired occasional bursts during the night, and was very active against our planes during the day. Our M.Gs fired 3,250 rounds harassing fire onto selected targets during the course of the night. Work of improving emplacements & shelters continued, work on dug-outs continued. Casualties wounded gas 1 O.R.	S.O.R.
	9-7-18		Bright & sunny early, rain fell all the afternoon and there were several showers during the evening. Visibility moderate. Enemy artillery displayed activity rather above usual, particularly at night. Our M.Gs fired	

Army Form C. 2118.

WAR DIARY
or
INTELLIGENCE SUMMARY.
(Erase heading not required.)

Instructions regarding War Diaries and Intelligence Summaries are contained in F.S. Regs., Part II and the Staff Manual respectively. Title pages will be prepared in manuscript.

Place	Date	Hour	Summary of Events and Information	Remarks and references to Appendices
Bus	9.7.16 (cont)		4,250 rounds harassing fire onto selected targets during the course of the night. A hostile plane flew over our Bus at about 7 p.m. & brought down one of our balloons. Work continued on dug outs & emplacements. Casualties nil.	cmR
I.23 central	10.7.16		Sunny early, very heavy rain fell at intervals from midday onwards, high wind, visibility fair. Battn H.Q. moved from Bus to camp at I.23 central. Move was completed by midday. During the evening "A" Coy relieved "C" Coy in the left sector of the Divisional Front, "C" Coy on relief took over positions vacated by "A" Coy. Relief was completed at 9.15 p.m. Enemy artillery activity slightly above normal during the night. An enemy plane flew over our lines at about 12.45 p.m. & brought down one of our balloons. Our M.G. fired 3,750 rounds on harassing fire onto selected targets during the course of the night. Work was continued on dug outs & emplacements. Casualties nil.	APP I cmR
	11.7.16		Dull & overcast all the morning, very high wind, heavy rain & storm during early evening. Rain fell throughout the night. Visibility poor. The activity of all hostile arms was normal. Our M.G. fired 3,500 rounds harassing fire during the night. Work was continued on new emplacements & dug outs. "D" Coy relieved "B" Coy in the right sector of the Divisional Front, "B" Coy on relief took over positions vacated by "D" Coy. Relief was completed at 6 p.m. Casualties Wounded 2 O.R.	APP I
	12.7.16		Stormy showers throughout the day, strong wind, visibility poor. Enemy artillery showed very little activity throughout the period under review. Enemy M.Gs were inactive. Our M.Gs fired 3,750 rounds onto selected targets during the course of the night	cmR

Army Form C. 2118.

WAR DIARY
or
INTELLIGENCE SUMMARY.
(Erase heading not required.)

Instructions regarding War Diaries and Intelligence Summaries are contained in F. S. Regs., Part II. and the Staff Manual respectively. Title pages will be prepared in manuscript.

Place	Date	Hour	Summary of Events and Information	Remarks and references to Appendices
I 23 Central	12-7-18		One enemy plane flew over our lines at 2 p.m. and was driven off by our M.Gs. The usual work was continued. Casualties nil.	ccR
	13-7-18		Sun shone at intervals, heavy rain fell during the early afternoon. Visibility good. Enemy activity normal, with the exception of hostile aircraft, which was very active; two of our observation balloons were brought down in flames about 8:30 p.m. Our artillery sent 4,250 rounds over during the night. Our M.Gs fired 4,250 rounds harassing fire during the night. 1.O.R. accidentally wounded.	ccR
	14-7-18		Dull & overcast, strong wind, rain fell at intervals during the day. Visibility poor. The present battle surface having completed their course of instruction were attached to three coys and a sudden movement proceeded to LOUVENCOURT. Situation on the front very quiet. Our M.Gs fired 4,250 rounds at allotted targets during the course of the night. Work was continued on dug-outs and emplacements, several new S.A.A. shelters were constructed and camouflaged. Casualties nil.	ccR
	15-7-18		Very hot, overcast, sun shone at intervals, visibility very good. Enemy artillery displayed normal activity. 30,000 rounds were fired to assist in carrying the operation carried out on our left by the N.Z. Division. Zero was at 4 p.m. and fire was continued from Zero until Zero + 30 mins. During the course of the night 5,000 rounds harassing fire was fired onto allotted targets. Enemy aircraft shewed slightly more activity than usual. The usual work was continued. Casualties nil.	ccR
AUTHIE	16-7-18		Very hot, heavy rain early in the morning, sun shone all the rest of the day. Visibility good.	

A5834 Wt.W4973/M687 750,000 8/16 D.D. & L. Ltd. Forms/C.2118/13.

WAR DIARY or INTELLIGENCE SUMMARY

Army Form C. 2118.

Place	Date	Hour	Summary of Events and Information	Remarks and references to Appendices
AUTHIE	16-7-18		Battalion HQ moved to AUTHIE, move was completed at midday. Enemy artillery showed slightly more activity than usual, particularly during the latter part of the day and the night. Enemy M.G. was active. Our M.G. fired 3,750 rounds harassing fire onto allotted targets during the night. Several enemy planes attempted to cross our lines but were driven back by our A.A. and M.G. gun. An enemy plane and observation balloon were brought down. The usual work was carried on day out and improvements. Casualties wounded 1 O.R.; accidentally wounded 1 O.R.	ref
	17-7-18		Rain fell during early morning and there was also a heavy shower at midday, otherwise sun shone all day, hot visibility good. Thunderstorm and rain during the evening. Vicinity of AUTHIE was bombed by hostile aircraft at about 2.30 am. Enemy artillery activity above normal, particularly during the evening. Our own aircraft were very active during the morning, an enemy observation balloon was brought down. Our M.G. fired 4,250 rounds onto selected targets during the course of the night. The usual work was continued. Casualties nil.	ref
BUS	18-7-18		Weather changeable, rain fell during the afternoon. Evening was fine + visibility was very good. Enemy artillery shelled BEAUSSART very heavily between 9.30 am – 11.30 am, otherwise there was no unusual activity. Our M. Coy fired 4,500 rounds harassing fire during the night. Enemy M.Gs were active. One enemy battalion broke loose + drifted in a Southerly direction. Work on dug-outs + improvements was continued. Enemy aircraft reported recently at BUS about 11.30 pm. Casualties No. 15 OR joined from Base Depot.	
	19-7-18		Sunny all day, visibility good, any hot + clear.	cR

WAR DIARY
or
INTELLIGENCE SUMMARY
(Erase heading not required.)

Army Form C. 2118.

Place	Date	Hour	Summary of Events and Information	Remarks and references to Appendices
BUS	19/7/18	(cont)	Enemy artillery quiet all day, very active at night during the operations which were carried out by 63rd R.N. Division on our right. Our M.Gs fired 33,500 rounds in conjunction with the artillery barrage covering the raid by 63rd Division. 4,500 rounds harassing fire were expended on selected targets during the course of the night. Shortly aircraft were more active than usual. Two enemy observation balloons were brought down in flames about 12.30 p.m. The usual work was continued. Casualties Killed 1 O.R.	ref
	20/7/18		Very hot + outlook, rain fell during the day, visibility poor. Enemy artillery were more active than usual. No harassing fire was undertaken by our M.Gs, enemy aircraft of our own kind. Our hostile planes crossed our lines about 10 p.m. but was driven off by our M.Gs. Work was continued on new dug outs and emplacements. Casualties NIL	ref
	21/7/18		Sunny, high wind, visibility good. C. Coy relieved D. Coy in the Right Section of the divisional front, D. Coy on relief took up positions vacated by C. Coy. The relief was completed at 9.15 am. B. Coy relieved A. Coy in the Left Section of the divisional front, A. Coy on relief took up positions vacated by B. Coy. The relief was completed at 6.30 p.m. Enemy artillery activity normal. Enemy M.Gs were active between 9.30 p.m. and 4 a.m. Several enemy planes attempted to cross our lines during the day, but were driven off by our M.Gs and A.A. guns. Work was continued in dug-outs + emplacements. Casualties wounded at duty 1 O.R. 6 O.R. joined from Base Depot.	APP II
	22/7/18		Sun, sunny at intervals, not visibility good, rain fell during the night.	ref

Army Form C. 2118.

WAR DIARY
or
INTELLIGENCE SUMMARY.
(Erase heading not required)

Instructions regarding War Diaries and Intelligence Summaries are contained in F. S. Regs., Part II. and the Staff Manual respectively. Title pages will be prepared in manuscript.

Place	Date	Hour	Summary of Events and Information	Remarks and references to Appendices
Bus	22-7-16 (cont)		Enemy artillery was quiet until about 11.45 a.m. when a barrage was put down on K.26 d. & K.27 d. which lasted until 12.10 p.m. After this there was considerable intermittent shelling for the remainder of the period under review. Enemy M.Gs fired during the hostile barrage on our trenches in K.26 b & 7 d. Two enemy planes flew over our lines about 8.15 p.m. but were driven off by A.A. gun & our own planes went very active. About 2.30 p.m. an enemy O.B. was brought down in flames. Work on emplacements improved & work continued on dug-outs Casualties wounded 1.O.R.	c.R.
	23-7-16		Rain fell practically all day, several very heavy downpours. Visibility poor. Enemy artillery was quiet during the morning. During the remainder of the day activity was normal. Enemy M.Gs displayed more activity than usual during the night. Our M. Go fired 2,000 rounds harassing fire onto K.29.a.50. (MATTHEW COPSE). There was very little aerial activity. Work was continued on dug-outs & gun positions. Casualties nil.	c.R.
	24-7-16		Dull & overcast several showers of rain, visibility moderate. Enemy artillery was very quiet until noon, after which the usual activity was displayed. Hostile M.Gs were fairly active during the night. Our own artillery carried out a bombard-ment on enemy trench systems between 12 noon & 3 p.m. A hostile plane attempted to cross our line during the evening, but was driven off by our M.Gs. The usual work was continued. Casualties, wounded at duty 1.O.R.	c.R.
	25-7-16		Dull, rain fell at intervals throughout the day, visibility poor. Enemy artillery activity normal. Enemy M.G. was more active than usual firing on roads and tracks during the night. The usual work on dug-outs & emplacements was continued. Casualties nil.	c.R.

WAR DIARY or INTELLIGENCE SUMMARY

(Erase heading not required.)

Army Form C. 2118.

Place	Date	Hour	Summary of Events and Information	Remarks and references to Appendices
BUS	26-7-18		Fine & sunny until mid day, rain fell during latter part of the day. Visibility fair. Rained all night. 3 Officers and 15 O.R. joined from Base Depot. Enemy artillery showed normal activity. Hostile M.G.'s were very active during the night. During the day M.G.'s were not very active. Firing on to roads and tracks behind our line. The M.G. work on dug outs & emplacements was continued. Casualties Nil.	ref
	27-7-18		Wet, rain fell nearly all day. Visibility bad. Enemy artillery was very quiet throughout the period under review. Enemy M.G. were less active than usual. Very little enemy activity in either side. Work on dug outs and emplacements was continued. Casualties Nil.	ref
	28-7-18		Dull and overcast, probably very low. Enemy artillery was very quiet. Area round COLINCAMPS and MAILLY MAILLET were lightly shelled with Gas Shells. Enemy M.G. fired about bursts over our positions. Tracks & roads during the night. Our M.G. fired 12,600 rounds harassing fire onto selected targets during the town of the night. Two enemy planes attempted to cross our lines during the day, but were driven off by our M.G. and A.A. guns. The usual work was continued. Casualties nil.	ref
	29-7-18		Sun shone during the early morning, dull & overcast during the rest of the day. Situation on the front very quiet during the day, considerable activity at night. Enemy fired a large number of gas shells into COLINCAMPS, MAILLY-MAILLET, BEAUSSART and COURCELLES from 11 pm onwards. Enemy M.G. was not more active than usual during the night, firing onto tracks and centres of movement. Our M.G. fired 4,000 rounds harassing fire onto selected targets during the night. Casualties Nil. The present battle surplus having completed their course of instruction were returned to their Coy and a similar number proceeded to HOUVENCOURT.	ref

Army Form C. 2118.

WAR DIARY
or
INTELLIGENCE SUMMARY.
(Erase heading not required.)

Instructions regarding War Diaries and Intelligence Summaries are contained in F. S. Regs., Part II. and the Staff Manual respectively. Title pages will be prepared in manuscript.

Place	Date	Hour	Summary of Events and Information	Remarks and references to Appendices
Bus	30.7.16		Sun and sunny, hot, very hazy, visibility very low. During the day enemy's counter battery fire was above normal, especially on batteries between SAILLY and COLINCAMPS. At 9 am a smoke barrage was put down as enemy great mine. At 9.30 am. Our M Gs fired 3000 rounds harassing fire during the night. Two enemy planes were brought down near COURCELLES during the morning. The usual work on dug-outs and emplacements was continued. Casualties killed 1 O.R., wounded Jan 2 O.R.	ceR
	31.7.16		Sunny, wet, visibility very low, very hazy. Enemy artillery showed greater activity than usual. Our MGs fired 5000 rounds into visible targets during the course of the night. Hostile aircraft was very active during the night, bombs were dropped in vicinity of COLINCAMPS, COURCELLES, SAILLY and MAILLY MAILLET. The usual work was continued. Casualties wounded 3gs. 1 OR	ceR

M. H. Tire
Lieut. Col.
Cmg 42nd Bn N.G.C

APP I

Copy No........

SECRET.

42nd. BATTALION, M.G.C. Order No. 21.

July 8th. 1918.

1. (a) 'A' Company will relieve 'C' Company in the Left Sector of the Divisional Front on the night 10th/11th. July.
   (b) 'C' Company on relief will take up positions vacated by 'A' Company.

2. (a) 'D' Company will relieve 'B' Company in the Right Sector of the Divisional Front on the night 11th/12th. July.
   (b) 'B' Company on relief will take up positions vacated by 'D' Company.

3. Details of relief will be arranged between O's. C. Companies concerned.

4. All maps, air photographs, harassing fire maps, S.O.S. arrangements, and working parties will be handed over on relief.

5. Completion of relief will be notified to Battalion H.Qrs. by Code Word "YORK".

6. ACKNOWLEDGE.

                                     CCRose   Capt. & Adjt.,
                              42nd. Battalion, M.G.Corps.

Distribution.
Copies 1 to 4. A.B.C. & D.Coys.
    "   No. 5. H.Q. 125th. Inf. Bde.
    "   " 6. " 126th. " "
    "   " 7. " 127th. " "
    "   " 8. 42nd. Division 'G'
    "   " 9. C.M.G.O.
    "   " 10. 'C' Coy. 57th. Bn. M.G.C.
    "   " 11 & 12. War Diary.
    "   " 13. File.

SECRET.   Copy No. 11

42nd. BATTALION, M.G.C. ORDER NO. 22.

July 19th. 1918.

1. (a). "C" Company will relieve "D" Company in the Right Sector of the Divisional Front on the night 20th/21st. July.
    (b). "D" Company on relief will take up positions vacated by "C" Company.

2. (a). "B" Company will relieve "A" Company in the Left Sector of the Divisional Front on the night 21st/22nd. July.
    (b). "A" Company on relief will take up positions vacated by "B" Company.

3. Details of relief will be arranged between O's. C. Companies concerned.

4. All maps, air photographs, harassing fire maps, S.O.S. arrangements, and working parties will be handed over on relief.

5. Completion of relief will be notified to Battalion H.Qrs. by Code Word "BRISTOL".

6. ACKNOWLEDGE.

                                       cc Rose   Capt. & Adjt.,
                                                  42nd. Battalion, M.G.Corps.

Distribution.
Copies 1 to 4. A.B.C. & D.Coys.
   "   No. 5. H.Q. 125th. Inf. Bde.
   "   " 6. "   126th. "   "
   "   " 7. "   127th. "   "
   "   " 8. 42nd. Division "G".
   "   " 9. C.M.G.O. IV Corps.
   "   " 10. "A" Coy. 57th. Bn. M.G.C.
   "   " 11 & 12. War Diary.
   "   " 13. File.

Confidential

Original

War Diary

of

42nd. Battalion

Machine Gun Corps.

(VOLUME VI)

From 1.8.18   To 31.8.18

Army Form C. 2118.

WAR DIARY
or
INTELLIGENCE SUMMARY.
(Erase heading not required.)

Instructions regarding War Diaries and Intelligence Summaries are contained in F.S. Regs., Part II. and the Staff Manual respectively. Title pages will be prepared in manuscript.

Ref SHEET 57D NE & SE
NW & SW
57C

Place	Date	Hour	Summary of Events and Information	Remarks and references to Appendices
Bus	1st		Sunny all day, hot, visibility fair. B Coy in the left sector of the Divisional front moved to H.Q. at T.23.a.80.45. A Coy relieved C Coy in the right sector of the Divisional front. C Coy on relief took up positions vacated by A Coy. Relief was completed at 8.30 p.m. Enemy artillery showed normal activity, HEBUTERNE, SAILLY and COLINCAMPS were shelled intermittently throughout the day. Enemy M.Gs showed no activity. Our M.Gs fired 3000 rounds harassing fire during the night. Hostile aircraft was more active than usual during the day, between 11 p.m. and mid-night bombs were dropped in the vicinity of MAILLY-MAILLET. Work on dug-outs was continued and emplacements generally improved. Casualties wounded 4 ors. 1.O.R. Rain fell practically all day, visibility poor.	APP. I
	2nd		D Coy relieved B Coy in the left sector of the Divisional front. B Coy on relief took up positions vacated by D Coy. Relief was completed at 5.30 p.m. Enemy artillery was very quiet. COLINCAMPS and HEBUTERNE were slightly shelled with gas shells. Hostile M.Gs were moderately active during the night. Our M.Gs fired 2,250 rounds harassing fire into STAFF COPSE and K.36.a.80.75. One enemy plane was brought down near MAILLY MAILLET. The usual work was continued. Casualties nil.	self APP. I
	3rd		Rain fell intermittently all day, visibility very poor. Enemy artillery showed normal activity. The usual areas being shelled. Enemy M.Gs were more active than usual during the night into RAILWAY AVENUE. Our M.Gs fired 2000 rounds harassing fire during the night into RAILWAY AVENUE. Two hostile planes crossed our lines at about 7.30 p.m. but were driven off by our M.G and 1A fire. A hostile observation balloon on our right was brought down in flames at 10.30 am. The usual work was continued. Casualties nil.	self
	4th		Fine and sunny, hot. Very heavy shower of rain at 4 p.m. Visibility fair.	self

Ar9921. Wt. W12839/M1298. 750,000. 11/17. D.D & L., Ltd. Forms/C2118/11.

WAR DIARY or INTELLIGENCE SUMMARY.

Army Form C. 2118.

Place	Date	Hour	Summary of Events and Information	Remarks and references to Appendices
BUS	4. (cont)		Enemy artillery was less active than usual at intervals during the day. Our own artillery was very active throughout the period under review. Our M.Gs fired 2,500 rounds harassing fire onto MATTHEW COPSE during the night. Aerial activity was practically nil. The usual work on dug-outs was continued and implacements were improved. Casualties Killed 3 O.R. Wounded 1 O.R.	ref
	5.		Rain fell practically all day, visibility very low. Enemy artillery displayed normal activity, the usual areas being shelled. Enemy M.G. were active than usual firing onto roads & tracks. Our M.Gs fired 5000 rounds on to LOUVENT FARM and K 28 d during the night. One enemy plane flew over our lines towards COLINCAMPS at 11 a.m. it was driven off by A.A. & our M.G. fire. Work camouflage improved, construction of dug-outs and implacements continued. Casualties nil.	ref
	6.		Dawn shower early, rain fell intermittantly during the remainder of the day, visibility poor. Enemy artillery was more active than usual. The windmill at MAILLY-MAILLET was heavily shelled from 10.30 am to midday. COLINCAMPS was also shelled. Enemy M.Gs were more active than usual. Our M.Gs fired 8,000 rounds harassing fire onto STAFF COPSE and K 34 d, K 6.1. 25 rifle aircraft displayed unusual activity; bombs were dropped in the vicinity of HEBUTERNE at 11.9 pm. The usual work was continued. Casualties Nil.	ref
	7.		Fine & sunny, visibility moderate. Enemy artillery very quiet during the day, rather active during the night especially in the vicinity of COLINCAMPS. Enemy M.Gs were more active than usual during the night firing onto our tracks and roads. Our M.Gs fired 8,000 rounds onto K 34 d, 7.1 and K 28. b & 2 during the night. Slight aircraft. The usual work was continued on dug-outs & implacements. Enemy aircraft showed abnormal	ref

Army Form C. 2118.

WAR DIARY
or
INTELLIGENCE SUMMARY.
(Erase heading not required.)

Instructions regarding War Diaries and Intelligence Summaries are contained in F.S. Regs., Part II. and the Staff Manual respectively. Title pages will be prepared in manuscript.

Place	Date	Hour	Summary of Events and Information	Remarks and references to Appendices
Bus.	8th		Dull, cool, visibility very low. Enemy artillery showed slightly more activity than usual. The windmill was again heavily shelled with gas shells from 6.30 p.m to 7 p.m. and at intervals during the night. Activity of enemy M.G. was normal. Green bullets were fired from the direction of SERRE. Our M.G. fired 13,000 rounds harassing gun onto selected targets opposite the Right Brigade sector in cooperation with the scheme to isolate VALLADE TRENCH. Hostile aircraft showed marked activity, bombs were dropped in the vicinity of SAILLY between 10 p.m and 1 a.m. The usual work was continued. Casualties NIL	self
	9th		Fine, strong wind, sun shone at intervals, visibility good. Hostile artillery normal. Shrapnel was fired over the windmill at MAILLY MAILLET during the morning. COLINCAMPS was slightly gas shelled at 9 p.m. Enemy M.G. were inactive. Our M.G. fired 13,000 rounds onto selected targets opposite the Right Brigade sector. Two hostile planes crossed our lines at 10.30 a.m. but were driven off by our M.G. & A.A. fire. The work on dug-outs & emplacements was continued. Casualties NIL	self
	10th		Sun shone all day, hot, visibility good. The present battle surplus having completed their course of instruction returned to their companies and a similar number proceeded to LOUVENCOURT. Activity of enemy artillery was below normal. COLINCAMPS AVENUE was slightly shelled with gas shells at about 11.30 p.m. Our M.G. fired 13,000 rounds onto selected targets opposite the Right Brigade Sector. Enemy M.G. were more active than usual. Hostile planes attempted to cross our lines at 11 p.m & 1 p.m but were driven off by our M.G. & A.A. fire. Gas bombs were dropped on our Trucks West of LA SIGNY FARM at about midnight. The usual work was continued. Casualties NIL	self
	11th		Fine & sunny, hot, visibility fair, only during to haze. Hostile artillery was more active than usual. COLINCAMPS, SAILLY and HEBUTERNE were continually shelled during the period under review. Enemy M.G. showed increased activity, particularly at "ALERT" &	

A.5834 Wt.W4973/M687 750,000 8/16 D.D. & L. Ltd. Forms/C.2118/13.

Army Form C. 2118.

WAR DIARY
or
INTELLIGENCE SUMMARY.
(Erase heading not required.)

Instructions regarding War Diaries and Intelligence Summaries are contained in F.S. Regs., Part II. and the Staff Manual respectively. Title pages will be prepared in manuscript.

Place	Date	Hour	Summary of Events and Information	Remarks and references to Appendices
BUS	11th (cont)		Our M.Gs. fired 5000 rounds harassing fire during the night and selected targets. Hostile aircraft showed considerable activity. Three planes were engaged by our M.Gs & driven off. The usual work was performed. Casualties NIL	C.E.P.
	12th		Our M.Gs. all day, but visibility poor owing to snow showers. C Coy relieved A Coy in the right sector of the divisional front. A Coy on relief took up positions vacated by C Coy. Relief was completed at 4.30 p.m. Hostile artillery displayed normal activity. The usual areas were shelled intermittently. Enemy M.G. fired occasional bursts throughout the night. Our M.Gs. fired 3000 rounds harassing fire and targets opposite the right brigade sector. A hostile plane dropped bombs near COLINCAMPS at 11.15 p.m. She went with an airpate and aeroplanes were returned. Casualties NIL	APP II C.E.P.
	13th		Fine — snowy but visibility good. B Coy relieved D Coy in the left sector of the divisional front. D Coy on relief took up positions vacated by B Coy. Relief was completed at 5 p.m. Normal activity was shown by hostile artillery. COLINCAMPS and LA SIGNY FARM were shelled intermittently. Throughout the period under review. Enemy M.Gs. were more active than usual during the night. Our M.Gs. fired 4000 rounds harassing fire onto targets in K.34.b. Several hostile planes attempted to cross our lines about 9 a.m. but were driven back by our M.G. + A.A. guns. The usual work was continued. Casualties NIL	APP II C.E.P.
	14th		Fine — sun shone all day; not visibility good. During the morning it was discovered that the enemy was returning opposite our front. Patrols were promptly sent out to obtain truth. At 7.30 p.m. pairs of guns were in position in the vicinity of STAFF COPSE, MATTHEW COPSE, MARK COPSE and JOHN COPSE, out of the line our infantry patrols went forward of the K.24. C.O.S. — EAST of SERRE — along SERRE - BEAUMONT HAMEL ROAD. There and gun were out up with the exception of intermittent shelling of the round...	C.E.P.

WAR DIARY
or
INTELLIGENCE SUMMARY.
(Erase heading not required.)

Army Form C. 2118.

Place	Date	Hour	Summary of Events and Information	Remarks and references to Appendices
BUS	14th (cont)		Erratic enemy M.G. were very active during the night. E. of SERRE hostile flares were seen and sent up at 3.20 p.m. Casualties NIL	ceR
	15th		Dull, wet, sun about all day, visibility good. O.C. "B" Coy moved forward 6 guns, 1 subsection to K.29.d.0.0., 1 subsection to K.35.b.1.8. and 1 section to K.35.c.2.4. O.C. "A" Coy moved forward 6 guns in STAFF, MATTHEW, MARK & JOHN. 1 section to K.35.c.2.4. O.C. "D" Coy ran 8 guns up to "D" Coy H.Q. in K.30.b.50. 1 section to K.30.c.8.2. 5000 rounds S.A.A. were sent further forward. 1.5 section to K.30.b.50. 1 section to K.30.c.8.2. 5000 rounds were fired by "C" Coy during the course of the day onto parties of the enemy who were holding up our patrols, many casualties were inflicted. At 5 p.m. C Coy moved 1 subsection from K.29.d.00 to K.36 central and 1 subsection from K.35.b.1.8 to K.36.c.8.7. Considerable activity was displayed by the enemy many artillery, the SERRE ridge, LA SIGNY FARM, STAFF COPSE and HEBUTERNE were shelled intermittently. Throughout the period enemy machine guns were very active, firing at our patrols. Hostile aircraft was inactive. Casualties NIL	ceR
	16th		Throughout the day fair, sunny, visibility poor. There was no substantial advance by our patrols during the morning. Parties of enemy in L.31 & L.32 were engaged & dispersed with many losses by our M.Gs. Hostile M.G. & snipers were very active. At noon our patrols withdrew to MUNICH TRENCH on account of hostile artillery fire. Our occupied thin advanced positions later. A subsection was moved from K.35.c.2.4 to Q.6.b central during the course of the evening. 2000 rounds were fired onto enemy concentrations in L.32 & L.31. 3000 rounds were fired at hostile movements during the course of the day. Hostile artillery & many Lights was less active than on the previous day. Enemy M.G.s shewed considerable activity against our patrols. Two hostile planes attempted to cross our lines at 7.30 p.m. but were driven off by our M.G. fire. Work upon new emplacements were continuing and shelters for men & S.A.A. were commenced. Casualties NIL	ceR
	17th		Dull sun, almost occasionally, strong wind, visibility poor	

WAR DIARY or INTELLIGENCE SUMMARY

Army Form C. 2118.

Place	Date	Hour	Summary of Events and Information	Remarks and references to Appendices
Bus	17	continued	Small parties of the enemy were engaged during the day on the ridge L.14.d and L.31.d by our M.Gs. The Regt veteran M.Gs fired 23,600 rounds onto L.32.b. L.33.a. L.21.d and L.27.c in cooperation with our artillery. The night section M.Gs fired 1900 rounds in support of infantry actions at 12.45 p.m. & 6 p.m. on several hostile M.Gs which tried to neutralize our guns were silenced. Hostile artillery was very active during N.Gs showed considerable activity. Two hostile planes which attempted to cross our lines at 6 p.m. were driven back by our M.G. + A.A. guns. In the right target sector 19 of C. Coys guns were moved up into positions in the vicinity of our old front line. The positions vacated by these guns were occupied by 16 of A Coys guns from the PURPLE LINE positions. New positions were constructed, existing positions were commenced & general improvements were continued. Work: new positions were constructed. Casualties NIL.	coff
	18		Sunny, visibility good, steady wind. Hostile artillery put down a heavy barrage along the SERRE RIDGE at 5 am. Shelled intermittently throughout the period under review. Our M.Gs engaged hostile snipers, M.Gs, + T.T Mis Suspected H.Qrs at L.32.b.2.b and O.P at L.31.d.0.9 went empts at intervals during the day by our M.Gs. The area L.26.d, L.27.c, L.32.b and L.33.d were constantly harassed with searching results. A large number of the enemy observed to be massing in sunken road L.26.a - L.32.b were engaged by four of our guns. The results could not be observed owing to ground mists. 25,000 rounds in all were fired. Hostile aircraft were very active between 3 am - 6 am. Casualties NIL.	coff
	19		Fine, dull visibility moderate. Hostile artillery showed marked counter-battery activity. The roads SERRE - MAILLY-MAILLET and SAILLY-COLINCAMPS were harassed at dusk. Our M.Gs engaged small parties of enemy in L.26.d., L.32.d., and R.2.a. and C with good results. Suspected enemy H.Qs and M.Gs were harassed throughout the night	

Army Form C. 2118.

WAR DIARY
or
INTELLIGENCE SUMMARY.
(Erase heading not required.)

Place	Date	Hour	Summary of Events and Information	Remarks and references to Appendices
BUS	19th (cont)		A total of 10,000 rounds were fired. Hostile M.G. went active from R 2.6. Enemy planes were active before 8 a.m. but were inactive afterwards. Forward emplacements were improved & shelters were constructed for men & S.A.A. Casualties NIL	ref
	20th		Clear, misty, dull, visibility poor until noon, when it considerably improved. Enemy went at night. The day was remarkably quiet except for occasional desultory shelling by hostile enemy artillery. Several hostile parties went engaged by our forward M.Gs with satisfactory results. Electric movement observed was below normal. Our M.G. fired at intimate through the night 20th/21st to neutralize the move of the Tanks coming up for the operations on the 21st. During the afternoon an 8 guns of A Coy were moved from their positions S.E. of COLINCAMPS to MUNICH TRENCH & 6 guns of the C Coy moved from positions in vicinity of sum an old great line and 2 guns from TITAN AVENUE & dug-outs S. of SERRE preparatory to going forward with attacking battalions. The 2 guns from TITAN AVENUE were relieved by A Coy. In the Left Brigade sector the 8 guns of B Coy in support were moved to dug-outs E. of SERRE preparatory to going forward with attacking battalions. The guns in MUNICH TRENCH and Q.U.G. and the guns in position in the vicinity of SERRE had our barrage lines for supporting the infantry. Casualties NIL	APP III ref
	21st		Very misty early. Sun shone later when it became very hot. At Zero hour (4.55 a.m.) a heavy barrage was put down by our artillery, & M.G's from positions in MUNICH TRENCH, E & S. of SERRE, & 8.6.a. Approx 150,000 rounds were fired by M.Gs during the barrage, which was indirect owing to heavy mist. The section of "B" Coy attached to the assaulting Battalion of the Left Brigade consolidated the first objective after it had been taken. As this phase of the operation in connection with the Right Brigade was not established, a defensive flank was therefore established by another section of "B" Coy which was in position at 10:15 a.m. when the assaulting battalion to which this section was attached moved forward and captured the final objective and a "handshake" had been effected with the Right Brigade. The guns were moved forward and placed	APP III

A7092. Wt. W12859/M1092. 750,000. 1/17. D.D & L., Ltd. Forms/C2118/12.

WAR DIARY
or
INTELLIGENCE SUMMARY.
(Erase heading not required.)

Army Form C. 2118.

Place	Date	Hour	Summary of Events and Information	Remarks and references to Appendices
BUS	21st (cont)		In position in the vicinity of the MIRAUMONT - PUISIEUX ROAD. The two sections of 'C' Coy attached to the 2nd Battns. Batteries of the Right Brigade moved forward where the objective had been taken. In each case the two guns of the section were ranged into position in rear of the final objective forming a rear section in Battalion reserve. Four guns of C Coy went forward from MUNICH TRENCH and distributed in depth in the vicinity of the PUISIEUX - BEAUCOURT ROAD (I-31). During the operations our gun of B Coy was damaged by shell fire. A hostile M.G. & team were captured. The gun was turned round and used against the enemy until it became damaged by shell gun. Hostile artillery fire was not heavy, but considerable resistance was offered by hostile M.G. firing from MIRAUMONT D Coy & two sections moved to K.25.a.1.5. The remaining 6 guns of D Coy in the PURPLE LINE were withdrawn from their positions to K.25.a.1.5. Casualties wounded 1 O.R. wounded at duty 2/Lieut R HOUGH (M.G.C.) and 2 O.R.	C.F.
	22nd		Misty early, then about later, may hot, visibility very good, misty at night. At 4.15 am the enemy launched a heavy counter attack against our recently won positions. The counter attack was preceded by a heavy bombardment by hostile artillery of all calibres, a small proportion of gas shells were used. The attack was entirely unknown up to our H.Q. 35000 rounds were fired and several hundred dead were afterwards counted in front of our M.G. positions. Our guns were instrumental in the capture of 217 prisoners. A Coy moved from vicinity of BUS to dug outs in J.4+5.6. during the course of the afternoon. Casualties killed 2 O.R. wounded 4 O.R. wounded Bgn 1 O.R.	C.F.
	23rd		Misty early, strong breeze mn, short hot, visibility fair. 3mm rain fell at about 11 pm. A Coy relieved C Coy in the right subsector, it lay in relief proceeded to dug outs in J.24 a.5.6. was completed at 7.30 p.m. B Coy fired 5000 rounds in conjunction with artillery into MIRAUMONT. This was done to prepare the way for fighting patrols. These guns were pushed	

WAR DIARY or INTELLIGENCE SUMMARY

Army Form C. 2118.

Place	Date	Hour	Summary of Events and Information	Remarks and references to Appendices
BUS	23rd (cont)		Forward Co. vicinity of BEAUREGARD DOVECOTE. Hostile M.G. and snipers were very active in their area. Very little hostile artillery fire. Casualties. Wounded 3 O.R. Wounded at duty 1 O.R.	CdR
K.35.a.04.	24th		Dull during morning, rain shower later, visibility poor. At 3 a.m. 1 section of D Coy was attached to B Coy and relieved 4 guns of the N.Z. M.G. Bn in the sector taken over by 126th Inf. Bde. on our immediate right. The gun positions taken over were in L.21.d. & L.23.c. Battn H.Q. closed at B.05. at 2 p.m. & reopened at the same hour at K.25.a.04. B Coy was relieved by D Coy during the evening. B Coy on relief proceeded to dug-outs in K.25.a.59. Relief was completed at 7 p.m. D Coy H.Q. were moved forward to L.27.b. & 0.35. D Coy's guns were then located as follows: 1 section in M.I.a.; 1 section M.S.a.; 1 subsection in L.23.d.; 1 subsection in L.23.c.; 1 subsection in L.28.d. After section in L.23.d.; 1 sub-section in L.21.d.; 1 subsection in L.28.c.; 1 subsection in L.28.d. After WARLENCOURT had been occupied A Coys guns were moved forward and disposed as follows for purposes of consolidation 1 subsection N/ + 1 subsection S of WARLENCOURT, 1 section W of WARLENCOURT in support, 2 sections in reserve in R.5.c.99. Casualties, Nil.	
K.25.a.04	25th		Fine all day, sunny, hot, visibility good. Heavy rain all night. Thunderstorm about 10 p.m. The divisions on our right & left having moved forward, 42nd Div was squeezed out and the division was concentrated as follows: 125th Inf. Bde. & C Coy in MIRAUMONT locality (C Coy moved from dugouts in T.24.d. & S.b. at 6 a.m. & reached MIRAUMONT at 9 a.m.); 126th Inf. Bde. & D Coy in WARLENCOURT and LOUPART WOOD locality; 127th Inf. Bde. + A Coy in PYS & IRLES locality. The present battle another having completed their count of instruction the personnel of B & C Coys were returned	CdR

WAR DIARY
or
INTELLIGENCE SUMMARY.
(Erase heading not required.)

Army Form C. 2118.

Place	Date	Hour	Summary of Events and Information	Remarks and references to Appendices
K.25.a.0.4.	25th	(cont)	to their companies and a similar number proceeded to LOUVENCOURT. Casualties NIL	A/R
	26th		From 3pm during the morning, fine during remainder of the day, visibility poor. B Coy left dugouts in K25.a.5.9 at 6 a.m. and moved to MIRAUMONT into divisional reserve. Casualties NIL	A/R
L.10.b.5.6.	27th		Fine all the morning, rain fell intermittently during the remainder of the day, visibility poor. Battn H.Q. moved from K.25.a.0.4. to L.10.b.5.6. Move was completed at 5.30 p.m. O.M. Stores and men B.H.Q. moved from K25.a.0.4 to MIRAUMONT during the afternoon. During the night the 42nd Bn M.G.C. relieved the 63rd Bn M.G.C. in the line. D Coy relieved the M.Gs in the right sector of the divisional front. Coy H.Q. were established at M.9.d.2.8. A Coy relieved the M.Gs in the left sector of the divisional front. Coy H.Q. were established G.3b.c.6.4. C Coy relieved support M.Gs. Company remained concentrated, Coy H.Q. were established at M.B.C.2.9. B Coy remained in divisional reserve at MIRAUMONT. Casualties NIL	
	28th		Showery all day, strong wind, visibility very low & improved occasionally towards evening. No shewing situation in the front was quiet, our artillery showed normal activity. The enemy artillery replied by the enemy was bursting shelling with guns of small calibre. Our aircraft were very active. Casualties Killed 2 O.R. Wounded 6 O.R. Wounded accidentally 1 O.R.	A/R
	29th		Sunny, very strong wind, visibility good. Hostile artillery displayed considerable activity especially against the trench areas, in all other respects the situation on the front was normal. Casualties NIL	A/R
G.29.d.9.6.	30th		Sunny all day, strong wind, visibility good, colder at night & rain fell. Battn H.Q. moved from L.10.b.5.6. to G.29.d.9.6. Move was completed at midday	

Army Form C. 2118.

WAR DIARY
or
INTELLIGENCE SUMMARY.
(Erase heading not required.)

Place	Date	Hour	Summary of Events and Information	Remarks and references to Appendices
G.29.d.9.6	30th (cont)		Owing to the wind that the enemy was retiring, the guns of A Coy were withdrawn from this hut and concentrated in the vicinity of LE BARQUE. D Coy then rearranged their guns to cover the DOWNWARD front. Enemy artillery showed considerable activity in harassing the back area, MIRAUMONT was shelled intermittently all day by a H.V. gun. an strong opposition was met with in the line RIENCOURT — BEAULENCOURT. A coy remained concentrated and did not move forward. Casualties Killed 1 O.R., Wounded 4 O.R.	cof
	31st		Rain fell during morning; am sheer later when visibility improved, strong wind. In the early morning A Coy relieved D Coy in the line; D Coy on relief proceeded to vicinity of LITTLE WOOD and remained concentrated. A Coys H.Q. remained at G.36.c.6.4. Hostile artillery shelled back areas; there was considerable aerial activity. Casualties NIL	cof

M.K. ....
Lieut Col.
Cmdg. 42nd Battn M G C

APP I

SECRET.

Copy No..........

42nd BATTALION, M.G.C. ORDER NO. 23.

July 31st. 1918.

1. (a). "A" Company will relieve "C" Company in the Right Sector of the Divisional Front on the night 1st/2nd. August.
   (b). "C" Company on relief will take up positions vacated by "A" Company.

2. (a). "D" Company will relieve "B" Company in the Left Sector of the Divisional Front on the night 2nd/3rd. August.
   (b). "B" Company on relief will take up positions vacated by "D" Company.

3. Details of relief will be arranged between O's. C. Companies concerned.

4. All maps, air photographs, harassing fire maps, S.O.S. arrangements, and working parties will be handed over on relief.

5. Completion of relief will be notified to Battalion H. Qrs. by Code Word "ENFIELD".

6. ACKNOWLEDGE.

W Ross
Capt. & Adjt.,
42nd. Battalion, M.G.Corps.

Distribution.
Copies 1 to 4. A,B,C, & D.Coys.
" "   No. 5. H.Q. 125th. Inf. Bde.
" "   " 6.   "   126th. "   "
" "   " 7.   "   127th. "   "
" "   " 8. 42nd. Division "G".
" "   " 9. C.M.G.O. IV Corps.
" "   " 10. "A" Coy. 63rd. Bn. M.G.C.
" "   " 11 & 12. War Diary.
" "   " 12. File.

SECRET.   App II   Copy No. 10.

42nd. BATTALION, M.G.C. ORDER NO. 25.

August 12th. 1918.

1.   (a).   'C' Company will relieve 'A' Company in the Right Sector of the Divisional Front on the 12th. August.
      (b).   'A' Company on relief will take up positions vacated by 'C' Company.

2.   (a).   'B' Company will relieve 'D' Company in the Left Sector of the Divisional Front on the night 13th/14th. August.
      (b).   'D' Company on relief will take up positions vacated by 'B' Company.

3.   Details of relief will be arranged between O's. C. Companies concerned.

4.   All maps, air photographs, harassing fire maps, S.O.S. arrangements and working parties will be handed over on relief.

5.   Completion of relief will be notified to Battalion H.Qrs. by Code Word "TORQUAY".

6.   ACKNOWLEDGE. (Companies only).

                                        CCRose   Capt. & Adjt.,
                                        42nd. Battalion, M.G.Corps.

Distribution.
Copies 1 to 4. A.B.C. & D.Coys.
   "   No. 5. H.Q. 125th Inf. Bde.
   "   " 6.   " 126th. "   "
   "   " 7.   " 127th. "   "
   "   " 8. 42nd. Division 'G'
   "   " 9. C.M.G.O. IV Corps.
   "   " 10 & 11. WAR Diary.
   "   " 12. File.

SECRET.   APP III   Copy No. 12

42nd. BATTALION, M.G.C. ORDER NO. 26.

August 20th. 1918.

Reference instructions issued regarding impending operations. Details have been given to all concerned.

The following general detail arranged in conjunction with both Brigades is given:-

OPERATIONS OF LEFT BRIGADE.

(a). 4 Guns go forward to assist in consolidating 1st. objective.
(b). 4 Guns go forward to assist in consolidating 3rd. objective.
(c). 4 Guns firing from N.E. of SERRE to give covering fire North of the LOZENGE and overhead fire.
(d). 4 Guns firing from S. of SERRE to give covering fire South of the LOZENGE and overhead fire.
(e). 8 Guns will fire from about MUNICH TRENCH sweeping the slopes and high ground in L.32.c. and d. South to Divnl. Boundary in R.2.
(f). 4 Guns firing from about Q.6.d. will harass L.31.d.

OPERATIONS OF RIGHT BRIGADE.

(a). 4 Guns attached to Left Battn.) for consolidation of 1st.
(b). 4 Guns attached to Right   "   ) and final objective.
(c). 8 Guns in MUNICH TRENCH. Fire at slopes between L.31 and L.32. (Southern limit line drawn East through R.1.b.6.5.) Commence firing at ZERO plus 50 and raise with advance of own troops.
(d). 4 Guns in Q.6.d. approximately. To fire at re-entrant in L.31.d. Commence firing at ZERO plus 50 and swing to the right as our own troops advance up the slopes. (Must not fire North of L.32.central.)
(e). 8 Guns in front of SERRE. Fire from ZERO plus 50 to ZERO plus 70 at L.31.d. to R.1.b.30.50. Raise at ZERO plus 70 to line L.32.c.50.95 to R.2.a.30.05. (half way to 1st. objective). When our own troops reach danger limit raise to 1st. objective. Cease fire when own troops are 2,000 yards in front of gun positions.

In Support 12 Guns.
In Divnl. Reserve 16 Guns.

CCRose   Capt. & Adjt.,
42nd. Battalion, M.G.C.

Distribution.
Copies 1 to 4. A.B.C. & D.Coys.
"   No. 5. H.Q. 125 Inf. Bde.
"   "   6. "   126t "   "
"   "   7. "   127 "   "
"   "   8. 42nd. Division "G".
"   "   9. O.M.G.C. IV Corps.
"   " 10. N.Z. M.G.Battn.
"   " 11. 21st. Bn. M.G.C.
"   " 12 & 13. War Diary.
"   " 14. File.
Issued at 5p.m. 20.8.18.

Confidential

(original)

War Diary

of

42nd Battalion Machine Gun Corps

Volume VII

from 1-9-18   To 30-9-18

WAR DIARY
or
INTELLIGENCE SUMMARY.
(Erase heading not required.)

Army Form C. 2118.

Place	Date	Hour	Summary of Events and Information	Remarks and references to Appendices
G29 d. 9.6	1.9.18		Cold – showy wind – dull – visibility fair – intermittent shelling – B Coy. moved from MIRAUMONT to H3d. central. Man was captured at 7.50 p.m. C Coy. moved into barrage positions W4 S of RIENCOURT. Casualties – wounded 1 O.R. –	ccf.
G29 d. 9.6	2.9.18		Showers – high wind – visibility fair – 127 Inf. Bde. attacked VILLERS-au-FLOS – The attack was supported by a barrage on the village provided by 16 guns of "C" Coy – 40,000 rounds were fired from zero to zero + 40; zero being at 5.15 a.m. After the barrage "C" Coy concentrated at N.S.d. Two sections of "A" Coy were attached to assaulting battalions and took up positions on section M.E. & on section S.E. of VILLERS-au-FLOS. One section formed a defensive flank on the right, the remaining 8 section being kept in Brigade Reserve. Enemy field guns and Machine Guns caused casualties amongst our own troops were engaged by A Coy forward guns with good effect, and by the covering fire of other guns our infantry were enabled to advance. Casualties – killed 1 O.R. – wounded 1 Officer, 6 O.R. –	
G29 d. 9.6	3.9.18		Fine – showers in the morning – windy until 6 p.m. visibility fair –	ccf.

WAR DIARY or INTELLIGENCE SUMMARY

Army Form C. 2118.

Place	Date	Hour	Summary of Events and Information	Remarks and references to Appendices
N5c 50.05	3.9.18 (cont.)		During the night of the 2nd/3rd Sept. the enemy retired from his positions East of VILLERS-au-FLOS. "C" Coy. attached 125 Bde. leaving bivouacs at N6d. leap-frogged through A Coy. attached 127 Bde., two sections being attached to forward Battalions, two sections being held in reserve at BARASTRE - Coy. H.Q. established at O15d 1.9.- The two forward sections came in contact with the enemy at P15 c, both sections came into action firing on enemy machine gun nests in LITTLE WOOD. "D" Coy. attached 126 Bde., moved into support. Coy. HQ. Established Ogd 4.7.- 3 sections attached to Battalions & one held in reserve at Coy HQ. "A" Coy. commenced at VILLERS-au-FLOS H.Q. remaining at N3c 7.6. "B" Coy. moved from H2d. central to BARASTRE, remaining in Bivouac at present. Move was completed at 7 p.m. - Q.M. Stores move from MIRAUMONT to H6 at 3.4, move was completed by 2 p.m. - The "Battle Surplus" became LOUVENCOURT at 6 a.m., & joined their Companies - Casualties - NIL.	
	4.9.18		Fine, bright, visibility good - During the morning the forward sections of "C" Coy. assisted the advance of 125 Bde. attending by engaging hostile M.G.'s & forward posts - A new line was established running East of YTRES. In the evening	

WAR DIARY or INTELLIGENCE SUMMARY

Army Form C. 2118.

Place	Date	Hour	Summary of Events and Information	Remarks and references to Appendices
	4.9.18 cont		Our Battalions carried out an attack on MEUVILLE-BOURTOUVAL by evening fire. Enemy artillery was very active. Long range H.V. guns shelled ROCQUIGNY & BUS during the day. BARASTRE was shelled from 6 to 8 pm with H.E. Battalion HQ moved to N5c 5.1. Casualties Wounded 8 O.R. Wounded at duty 1 O.R.	c.c.R.
N5c 5.1.	5.9.18		Quiet during the morning. Enemy in the afternoon visibility fair. At 4.30 p.m. the Infantry attacked the high ground east of NEUVILLE-BOURTOUVAL. "B" Coy covered "C" Coy in covering the advance of 125 Bde by procuring a barrage with 16 guns on PROUD & PESTLE Trenches from Zero Hours to Zero + 69 Mins. Approximately 70,000 rounds were fired from our guns. Casualties. Killed 2 O.R. Wounded 1 Officer (2/Lt. BARNETT. J., M.G.C.) 1 O.R. Wounded at duty 2 O.R.	c.c.R.
H.6.d.3.5.	6.9.18		Fine, very hot. Visibility fair. Westerly wind till 6 p.m. The 42nd Division was relieved in the Line by the New Zealand Division on the morning of the 6th. The Company No M.G. Battalion relieved "C" Coy in the Line. On relief "C" Coy continued with 125 Bde Group & proceeded to the area. Coy HQ was established at M.3d.2.9. Command of the Divisional area having passed to GOC NZ Division at midnight 5th–6th. "B" Coy relieving "A" Coy and marched to 127 Bde. area at WARLENCOURT. Coy HQ Truro	

Army Form C. 2118.

WAR DIARY
or
INTELLIGENCE SUMMARY.
(Erase heading not required.)

Place	Date	Hour	Summary of Events and Information	Remarks and references to Appendices
M6 a. 3.6.	7.9.18		Established at M9 d.2.9. "B" Coy. & 126 Bat. Group marched to LE BARQUE area. Coy. H.Q. were established at M6.b.1.1. "A" Coy's relieving "B" Coy. in divisional reserve moved to M6 a.9.2. Battalion H.Q. moved from N5c.5.1. to LE BARQUE (M6a.3.5). Casualties - Nil.	ccf.
			Fine, warm, westerly breeze. Visibility good. The CO held a Conference of Company Commanders at B.H.Q. to discuss recent operations. This was followed by a Conference attended by the C.O. & O.C. Companies at B.H.Q. on the Battle of RIENCOURT. The Coys. spent the day washing & cleaning up. Casualties - Nil.	ccf
M6 d. 3.5	8.9.18		Dull, mild & showery. Visibility bad. The Coys spent the day resting. Casualties - Nil.	ccf
M6 d. 3.5	9.9.18		Rain at intervals, westerly wind, visibility good. During the morning a tactical scheme was carried out by "A" Coy. in the presence of all officers & senior NCOs of the Battalion, to demonstrate the employment of Machine guns in cooperation with Infantry fighting patrols. The remainder of the day were spent in cleaning up & overhauling equipment. Casualties - Nil.	ccf.

A5834 Wt.W4973/M687 750,000 8/16 D. D. & L. Ltd. Forms/C.2118/13.

Army Form C. 2118.

WAR DIARY
or
INTELLIGENCE SUMMARY.
(Erase heading not required.)

Instructions regarding War Diaries and Intelligence Summaries are contained in F.S. Regs., Part II. and the Staff Manual respectively. Title pages will be prepared in manuscript.

Place	Date	Hour	Summary of Events and Information	Remarks and references to Appendices
M6d.3.5.	10.9.18		Strong westerly wind. Shower - cloud at about afternoon. Heavy rain during the night. Usual training. Training was carried out in accordance with Appendix I. Casualties. Accidentally wounded. 1 O.R.	APP I cef
M6d.3.5	11.9.18		Strong westerly wind. Showery - visibility fair. Companies carried out training with the Bugler Bugles to which they were attached. Casualties - Nil.	cef
M6d.3.5	12.9.18		Cloudy. Rained later part of the day. Dull, visibility poor. Training with Infantry battalions was postponed owing to the weather. Casualties - Nil.	cef
M6d.3.5	13.9.18		Cloudy. Bright afternoon, visibility fair. Companies carried out training with Infantry Battalions in the morning. There was a Cross-country run in the afternoon which was won by "A" Coy. with 110 points, "B" Coy. second with 89 points. Casualties - Nil.	cef
M6d.3.5	14.9.18		Dull + windy - visibility fair in the morning, poor in the afternoon. In the morning Coy. did training with Infantry Battalions. A & D Coys. 1 Batt. H.Q. played football against the 1/105 Howitzers in the afternoon.	cef

A.5834 Wt.W4973/M687 750,000 8/16 D.D.&L.Ltd Forms/C.2118/13.

WAR DIARY
or
INTELLIGENCE SUMMARY.
(Erase heading not required)

Army Form C. 2118.

Place	Date	Hour	Summary of Events and Information	Remarks and references to Appendices
M6d.3.5			H.T.C. won by 2 goals to nil. (Casualties N/K.)	cef
M6d.3.5	15.9.18		Fine and warm. Visibility good. It being Sunday there was no training. Church parades in the morning. Casualties N/K.	cef
M6d.3.5	16.9.18		Very fine all day. Visibility good. Heavy thunderstorm during the night. Coys carried out training with Infantry Battalions. Casualties N/K.	cef
M6d.3.5	17.9.18		Fine & warm during the day. It rained heavily during the night. Visibility good. Coys trained in co-operation with Infantry Battalions. Casualties N/K.	cef
M6d.3.5	18.9.18		Fine & bright. Visibility good. Training in the morning with Brigades. The C.O. gave a conference of O.C. Coys in the evening. Casualties N/K.	cef
M6d.3.5	19.9.18		Fine, visibility good. Coys carried out training in the morning operating with Infantry Battalions. Casualties - Accidentally wounded 1 O.R.	cef
M6d.3.5	20.9.18		Cold & dull - Visibility good - "D" Coy plus one Section "A" Coy attached	cef APP II

126

WAR DIARY or INTELLIGENCE SUMMARY

Army Form C. 2118.

Place	Date	Hour	Summary of Events and Information	Remarks and references to Appendices
			126 Brigade moved up & took over forward positions in the line from the 37th Batt M.G.C., preliminary to a Divisional relief of the 21st Corps H.Q. were established at Q2d 6.4. "C" Coy carried out the usual harassing – "A" & "B" Coys. prepared for the relief. Casualties – NIL	ccf
Q 31.c. 4.7.	21.9.18		Showery & windy in the morning, brightened up in the afternoon. Visibility poor – The 42nd Division relieved the 37th Division in the line – Left Sector, 4th Corps. Battalion H.Q. moving from H.6.d.3.5. was established in VELU WOOD at Q.31.c.4.7. new Bound. completed at 3 p.m. "B" Coy moved from H.9.a.85.90. establishing Coy. H.Q. near BERTINCOURT at P.2.d.3.8. Guns of this Coy. (attached 127 Bde) were put into Support positions. "A" Coy Line Section moved from H.6.d.1.9 into Divisional Reserve in vicinity of LEBUCQUIERE, Coy H.Q. being established at I.29.6.7.1. Shire was considerable back area shelling with H.V. guns in the afternoon. Casualties – Killed 2 O.R., M.S.C., 1 O.R., R.E.	App II
I.29.d.4.3.	22.9.18		Wind from the West – Rainy & dull – Visibility poor. "C" Coy (attached 125th Inf. Bde.) moved up into the line in the vicinity of LEBUCQUIERE, Coy H.Q. being established at I.24.d.1.1. the move was completed at 12.10 p.m.	ccf

WAR DIARY
or
INTELLIGENCE SUMMARY.

Army Form C. 2118.

Place	Date	Hour	Summary of Events and Information	Remarks and references to Appendices
I.29.d.4.3.	12th (cont)		Both H.Q. moved to I.29.d.4.3. The area was completed at midday. Hostile artillery was active throughout the period under review; HAVRINCOURT WOOD, HERMIES and TRESCAULT were shelled by guns of large calibre. FERNY WOOD was slightly shelled with gas. H.V. guns were very active in the VELU-BERTINCOURT area. Hostile M.G. displayed increased activity in sniping any visible movements of our troops. Enemy aircraft showed increased activity. Casualties Wounded ___ I.O.R. Wounded Sgn I.O.R.	cop
I.36.d.8.1.	23rd		Dull, strong wind, rain fell during the afternoon. Visibility was poor but improved slightly during the early evening. Both H.Q. moved to I.36.d.8.1. The area was completed at 3.p.m. Hostile artillery was considerably less active than on the 22nd. HAVRINCOURT WOOD was shelled intermittently during the day. LONG VALLEY and MATHESON ROAD were equally shelled throughout the period under review. Hostile H.V. guns were very active in the VELU-BERTINCOURT area. Our own artillery and aircraft displayed very considerable activity. Casualties Wounded 1/O.R. Wounded Sgn 113 O.R. Injured gas slightly (S.I.) 1 O.R.	cop
	24th		Strong wind, dull, several showers of rain 1 rain storm at intervals. Visibility poor. Enemy artillery was active, the usual areas were shelled. Two enemy observation balloons were brought down in flames at 2 p.m. During the night our M.G. fired 2,500 rounds at the road running N.E. through K.36.b. and 1000 rounds onto sunken road in K.36.a. Casualties NIL	cop

WAR DIARY
or
INTELLIGENCE SUMMARY.
(Erase heading not required.)

Army Form C. 2118.

Place	Date	Hour	Summary of Events and Information	Remarks and references to Appendices
I.36.d.5.1.	25ᵗʰ		Strong wind, dull, rain fell during the morning, visibility poor. 2 Sections of "A" Coy relieved the night 2 Sections of "D" Coy at dusk. "D" Coy then concentrated in the vicinity of STAR TRENCH. Battle outfitting was quiet during the day, but showed considerable activity at night at 4 p.m. about 50 g.m. shells were fired into TRESCAULT. Hostile aircraft was very active. Hostile M.G. displayed increased activity firing into roads & tracks behind our lines. Several parties of enemy were successfully engaged in Q.5.a. and casualties were inflicted. Casualties NIL	J.P.
	26ᵗʰ		Sun shone at intervals, when visibility was good. Rain fell at night. During the course of the day "A" Coy moved to BUNG ALLEY and 8 guns of SHERWOOD AVENUE intact barrage position had already been prepared; Coy H.Qrs were established at Q.8.d.6.4. and near Coy H.Qrs and transport lines moved to P.9.c.2.6. "B" Coy moved up and concentrated in the vicinity of FERN WOOD; Coy H.Qrs were established during the evening at K.33. a.3.8. and near Coy H.Qrs. Coy/Lieu with transport lines were left at T.2.d.4.7. During the afternoon "C" Coy moved up and concentrated in SNAP RESERVE TRENCH; Coy H.Qrs were established at Q.10.b.85.30. "D" Coy carried barrage position in STAR TRENCH and KANGAROO AVENUE. Hostile artillery displayed normal activity, the vicinity of RUYAULCOURT was mainly shelled during the afternoon great aerial activity was shown by both hostile & our own aircraft. Two of our observation balloons were brought down in flames at 5 p.m. Hostile M.V. guns active too. Weak areas within Divy. Casualties Killed 1 O.R. Wounded 1 O.R	J.P.

WAR DIARY or INTELLIGENCE SUMMARY.

Army Form C. 2118.

(Erase heading not required.)

Place	Date	Hour	Summary of Events and Information	Remarks and references to Appendices
I.36.d & I.1.	27th		Rain during early morning and above at intervals throughout the day. Visibility good. The 42nd Divn attacked in the morning of Sept 27th. The attack of the 125th Bde on the right was covered by 16 guns of "A" Coy. 51000 rounds were fired from positions in BUNG ALLEY and SHERWOOD TRENCH until the slopes in K.16 and along HIGHLAND RIDGE. The attack of the 127th Bde on the left was covered by 16 guns of D Coy from positions in STAR TRENCH. 62000 rounds went from the HINDENBURG front line system in K.36. The barrage was maintained from ZERO + 19th until the infantry had gained the second objective. C Coy affiliated to 125th Inf Bde assembled with pack animals in SNAP RESERVE, only one gun of the Coy was sent forward owing to the situation being obscure. The gun moved to a position W. of BEAUCAMP and assembled for many to the enemy before it was knocked out. On the left B Coy moved forward with pack animals from the assembly position at FENY WOOD. This Brown line was consolidated at K.34.b.8.9. The remaining three outfits consolidated at the following points K.36.a & 7.5. L.31.c.4.4. & K.30.c.4.3. During the afternoon 3 guns at L.31.c engaged two enemy field guns which were in action at Q.6.9.77 Guns were stationed and casualties inflicted and two MGs carrying the guns were observed. Parties of enemy were fired on with effect along the sunken road in L.31.c.7.A. Casualties Killed 9 OR, Wounded 3 MOR, wounded at duty 2 FS section + 1 OR wounded + missing 1 OR	APP III
	28th		Dull during morning, heavy rain fell at midday, including fair. C Coy went forward with pack animals to consolidate the Brown line after the attack at 2.30 am. HIGHLAND RIDGE was promptly occupied by one section at RHONDDA POST and 1 section at R.14 & 9.0. 2 sections remaining in depth on the Yellow line. By 3 pm 1 section from the yellow line had moved onto WELSH RIDGE at R.9.c central. B Coy advanced down to the Brown line consolidating points on yellow 2 guns at L.32.b.9.5, 2 guns at L.27.d.1.1, 4 guns at R.2.a.8.8. That gun engaged the hostile field gun being withdrawn complete with teams by 6 horses along road in L.23.b.r.d., killing 6 horses. Good shooting was obtained on the enemy falling back from the Brown line to WELSH RIDGE. At 11.30 am 1 section of B Coy consolidated	

WAR DIARY or INTELLIGENCE SUMMARY.

Army Form C. 2118.

Place	Date	Hour	Summary of Events and Information	Remarks and references to Appendices
I 34 d & I	28th (cont)		WELSH RIDGE at R.30 central and the remaining sections were distributed covering the valley E. of the Bent line. During the afternoon B Coy captured 2 M.G. & 50 prisoners and were severely repulsed by the 2 Irish Gun machines down. One section of D Coy to operate with the 1/10th Manchr. Regt. in exploring avenues on WELSH RIDGE. Coy H.Q. & 3 sections went round forward to L.31.b.35. Casualties Wounded 1.O.R.	ref.
	29th		Cold & sunny early, rain fell during the afternoon & evening. Strong wind, visibility good at 3 am the N.Z. Division completed passing through the 42nd Divn, which then came into camps. Reserve. During the day, A Coy concentrated at Q.5.d.4.4 & moved to P.5.d.1.3 B Coy concentrated at K.33.d. & moved to P.5.d.1.3 C Coy concentrated at Q.10 central & moved to Q.11.a & moved to Q.5.d.4.4. Casualties NIL	ref.
	30th		Cold, dull, strong wind, visibility poor. The day was devoted by all Coys to cleaning up & overhauling guns & equipment. A conference was held by the C.O. & the recent fighting & lessons learnt therefrom were discussed. Casualties NIL	ref.

....
Lieut Col
Cmg 42nd Battn M.G.C.

APP I

TRAINING PROGRAMME.

For 10th. September 1918.

Unit.	Map Ref. of Place.	Time.	Nature of Training.	Remarks.
42nd Battn. M.G.C.	M.6.a. and M.9.a.	9a.m. - 9.45a.m.	Coy. Parade. Coy. Inspection. Steady Drill. Saluting.	
	- do -	10a.m-10.45a.m.	Physical Training.	
	M.6.a. and M.3.d.	11a.m. - 1p.m.	Advanced Guard Schemes. Co-operation with Fighting Patrols.	
	M.6.a. and M.9.a.	2p.m. - 4p.m.	Musketry and Recreational Training.	

9.9.18.

Sd/ R.C.Guinness, Major for O.C.
42nd. Battalion, M.G.Corps.

SECRET.   APP II   Copy No......16......

42nd. BATTALION, M.G.C. ORDER NO. 27.

September 18th. 1918.

1. 42nd. Battalion, Machine Gun Corps will relieve 37th. Battalion, Machine Gun Corps in the Left Sector of the IV Corps Front on September 20th., 21st., and 22nd.

2. The Boundaries of the 37th. Division are as follows:-
    Southern Boundary. Q.7.central. Q.9.c.0.0. thence due East.
    Northern Boundary. K.33.central. K.28.d.0.0. thence due East.

3. 127th Inf. Brigade will place one Battalion at the disposal of 126th. Inf. Brigade from midnight 19th/20th. September. This Battalion will not be put into the line and will only be used in case of tactical emergency.

4. 'D' Company, 42nd. Battalion, M.G.C. plus 1 Section of 'A' Company, will move up to relieve one Company and one Section of the 37th. Battalion, M.G.C. in the Line by omnibus leaving M.G.d.2.4. at 1p.m. on 20th. instant.   Relief to be complete by 5a.m. 21st. instant.

5. 'B' and 'C' Companies, 42nd. Battalion, M.G.C. will move with their Brigade Groups into Support and Reserve respectively in accordance with attached March Table.

6. 'A' Company, 42nd. Battalion, M.G.C. less one Section will move in accordance with attached March Table.
    O.C. 'A' Company will make arrangements with the Company Commander concerned of the 37th. Battalion, M.G.C. re time of relief etc.

7. Completion of moves and reliefs will be reported to Battalion H.Qrs. by Code Word "HECTOR".

8. Battalion H.Qrs. will open at ~~L.36.d.8.1.~~ J.31.c.3.8. at 5p.m. on 21st. instant.

9. ACKNOWLEDGE. (M.G. Companies only.)

Major for O.C.
42nd. Battalion, M.G.C.

Distribution.
Copies 1 to 4. A.B.C. & D.Coys.
"   No. 5. H.Q. 42 Divn. 'G'
"   "   6. H.Q. 126th Inf. Bde.
"   "   7. 37th Bn. M.G.C.
"   "   8. C.M.G.C. IV Corps.
"   "   9. Quartermaster.
"   "   10. Signal Officer.
"   "   11 & 12. War Diary.
"   "   13. File.

APP III

In accordance with the views of B.G's. C. 125th. and 127th. Brigades the Machine Gun arrangements will be as follows:-

'B' Company and 'D' Company, 42nd. Battn. M.G.C. will co-operate with the 127th. Brigade.

'A' Company and 'C' Company, 42nd. Battn. M.G.C. will co-operate with the 125th. Brigade.

'D' Company will provide covering fire during the advance of the 127th Brigade upon UNSEEN TRENCH, UNSEEN SUPPORT and MOLE TRENCH in accordance with attached trace.

On completion of above task O.C. 'D' Company will send 8 Guns forward to consolidate CHAPEL WOOD SWITCH and this Company will once more become available to co-operate with the 126th. Brigade.

'A' Company will provide covering fire to cover the advance of the 127th Brigade and the 125th Brigade in accordance with attached trace; fire being mainly brought to bear on slopes of BOAR COPSE VALLEY in K.36.c. Q.6.a. Q.5.c. and going gradually East, also on BEAUCAMP RIDGE assisted by 5th. Battalion, M.G.C.

On completion of above task O.C. 'A' Company will send 8 Guns forward to consolidate SHAFTESBURY AVENUE, and this Company will be in Divisional Reserve.

'B' Company will co-operate with the 127th. Brigade (H.Qrs. Q.3.b.6.2.) for purposes of consolidation and it is hoped that it may be possible to push these four Sections (1 Company) through with 8 Pack animals quickly to the undermentioned objectives without it being necessary for them to fight their way forward.

The Officer Commanding 'B' Company, 42nd. Battn. M.G.C. and the four Sections will remain with the Officer Commanding the 7th. Battn. Manchester Rgt. and O.C. 'B' Company will detail his Sections to go forward and consolidate the four objectives in accordance with the reports received about the progress of the attack by O.C. 7th. Manchester Regt.

The following points will be consolidated by the 4 Sections of 'B' Company:-

1. L.32.b.3.7.
2. R.2.a.8.9.
3. K.36.b.8.9.
4. L.31.c.2.2.

'B' Company will assemble near FEMY WOOD, K.34.d.4.9. prior to the attack.

'C' Company will co-operate with the 125th. Brigade (H.Qrs. MORTAMARE Q.8.d.2.5.) for purposes of consolidation and it is hoped that it may be possible to push these four Sections (1 Company) through with 8 Pack animals quickly to the undermentioned objectives without it being necessary for them to fight their way forward.

The Officer Commanding 'C' Company, 42nd. Battn. M.G.C. and the four Sections will remain with the Officer Commanding the 8th. Battn. Lancashire Fus. and O.C. 'C' Company will detail his Sections to go forward and consolidate the four objectives in accordance with the reports received about the progress of the attack by O.C. 8th. Lancs. Fus.

P.T.O.

The following points will be consolidated by the four Sections of
'C' Company:-
1. R.8.a.1.9.
2. R.7.d.2.9.
3. Q.6.b.0.6.
4. Q.12.d.central.
'C' Company will assemble in SNAP RESERVE Q.10.d. and Q.16.b.
prior to attack.

SECRET.
Copy No......

AMENDMENT TO 42nd. BATTALION, M.G.C. ORDER NO. 27.

September 20th, 1918.

1. Reference Para. 2. Divisional Southern Boundary is amended to read as follows:-
    PLACE MORTIER (inclusive to Left Divn.) to BEAUCAMP (inclusive to Right Divn.)

2. Para. 8 - Location of Battalion H.Qrs. should be amended to read J.5L.c.3.8.

3. ACKNOWLEDGE. (M.G. Companies only.)

A.R.C.Bunting

Major for O.C.
42nd, Battalion, M.G.C.

Distribution.
As per Order No. 27.

March Table to Accompany 42nd Battn. M.G.C. Order No. 27.

Date	Unit	From	To	Relieves	Remarks
September 20th	D Coy 42nd Battn. M.G.C. 1 Section 'A' Coy 42nd Battn. M.G.C.	THILLOY Area	Line	1 Coy and 1 Section of 31st Battn. M.G.C.	Rly bus from THILLOY to RUYAULCOURT. Relief to be complete by 5 am 21st September
	126 Inf Bde Group less M.G. Coy plus 1 Battn. 127 Inf Bde.	THILLOY - LA BARQUE Area	VELU - BEUGNY LEBUCQUIERE Area	111th Inf Bde Group	Any route.
21st	127 Inf Bde Group less 1 Battn	WARLENCOURT Area	Support RUYAULCOURT Army Group less 1 Battn.	112th Inf Bde Group less 1 Battn.	Any route.
	114th Machine Gun Coy. (Pioneer Battn.)	FREMICOURT	Pys. Gr.	9th N. Staffs (Pioneer) Battn.	To move under orders of C.R.E.
	'A' Coy less 1 Section 42nd M.G. Battn.	THILLOY	VELU	1 Coy 31st Battn. M.G.C.	
	112nd D.H.Q.	RIENCOURT I.36.d.9.1.	I.36.d.9.1.	31st D.H.Q.	Move to be complete by 5 am.
21/22nd	126 Inf Bde Group less M.G. Coy plus 1 Battn.	VELU - BEUGNY LEBUCQUIERE Area	Line	63rd Inf Bde Group less M.G. Coy plus 1 Battn.	All arrangements to be made between B.G.C. concerned
22	125 Inf Bde.	PYS Area	VELU - BEUGNY LEBUCQUIERE Area (Reserve)	63rd Inf Bde Group	Relief to be complete by 5 am.

APP V

42nd. BATTALION, M.G.C.
TRAINING PROGRAMME FOR THURSDAY, OCTOBER 31st. 1918.

'A' Company.	'B' Company.	'C' Company.	'D' Company.
08.45. Coy. Parade.	08.45. Coy. Parade.	08.45. Coy. Parade.	08.45. Coy. Parade.
09.00 - 13.00. %Squad Drill. I.A. Combined Drill. Section Tactical Exercises.	09.00 - 09.45. Squad Drill.	09.00 - 09.30. Squad Drill.	09.00 - 09.45. Belt Inspection and Cleaning.
	09.45 - 10.45. Immediate Action.	09.30 - 10.15. P.T.	10.00 - 10.45. P.T.
	11.00 - 13.00. Section Tactical Exercises.	10.30 - 13.00. Section Tactical Exercises.	11.00 - 12.30. Section Tactical Exercises.

A F T E R N O O N - RECREATIONAL TRAINING.

All the above training will be carried out in the vicinity of billets at BEAUVOIS, except training marked % which will be carried out at I.4.c.

T.P.2.
30.10.18.

Major for O.C.
42nd. Battalion, M.G.C.

SECRET

APP III

Reference Sheet's 57cNE & SE 1/20000

Identification Trace for use with Artillery Maps.

G.S.G.S. 2085.

Tracing taken from Sheet _____ of the 1: _____ map of _____

Signature _____
Date _____

NOTE.—(1). These tracks are intended to facilitate the communication of information as to the position of targets, which have been located on a squared map.
(2) The squares on this trace are 500 yards in length on the 1/20,000 scale, 1,000 yards in length on the 1/20,000 scale, and 2,000 yards in length on the 1/40,000 scale.
(3) The squares on the trace are fitted to the squares of the map showing the targets, which are then drawn on the trace. Sufficient letters and numbers must also be added to enable the recipient to place the trace in the correct position on his own map. A little detail may also be traced, but this is not essential. The name and scale of the map to which the trace refers must be always given. The trace can be used for the 1/10,000, 1/20,000, or 1/40,000 scale.

LEGEND
Barrage of Hep.Coy
D" Right Coy
Right Sub Sec.ⁿ Consolidation Section 4 Guns
Left Sub-Sec.ⁿ Consolidation Section 4 Guns

BOUNDARY
DIVISIONAL BOUNDARY
BRIGADE BOUNDARY
DIVISIONAL

Arrives Z+352
Arrives Z+324
Leaves Z+320
Arrives Z+342 Also / Arrives Z+306 R 318
Arrive Z+332 & 312
Leaves Z+330
Leaves Z+330
Arrive Z+338 Leaves Z+346
Leaves Z+310
Z+8 Z+230
Arrive Z+334 Leave Z+334
Arrives Z+198
Leaves +198
Arrive Z+190
Leave Z+143
Leave Z+200 & 214
Arrive Z+80

42nd BATTALION,
MACHINE GUN
CORPS.
No. _____ Date _____

Confidential

(Original)

WAR DIARY

of

42nd Battalion Machine Gun Corps

Volume VIII

From 1-10-18 To 31-10-18

Army Form C. 2118.

WAR DIARY
or
INTELLIGENCE SUMMARY.
(Erase heading not required.)

Instructions regarding War Diaries and Intelligence Summaries are contained in F. S. Regs., Part II. and the Staff Manual respectively. Title pages will be prepared in manuscript.

Place	Date	Hour	Summary of Events and Information	Remarks and references to Appendices
I.3.b.d.8.1.	1st		Rain fell during early morning, sun shone all day cold, visibility fair. Companies spent the day sorting, cleaning up & overhauling equipment. Recreational Training took place. Casualties NIL	ref
	2nd		Fine but dull, cold, visibility fair, rain fell during afternoon & evening. Companies spent the day sorting and cleaning & overhauling guns & equipment. Recreational Training took place during the afternoon. Casualties NIL	ref
	3rd		Sun shone all day, visibility good, warmer. The C.O. inspected Coys at the following times: B Coy at 09.30, A Coy at 10.15, C Coy at 11.30 and D Coy at 12.15. Training was carried out in accordance with Appendix I. A draft of 30 O.R.'s (reinforcements) joined from Machine Gun Corps Base Depôt. The C.O. held a Coy. Commanders Conference at B.H.Q. at 16.00 to discuss forthcoming arrangements in forthcoming operations. Casualties NIL	APP I
	4th		Dull showery morning, cold, visibility poor. Coys trained during the morning with the infantry of the Brigades, to which they are affiliated. In the afternoon was devoted to recreational training. A draft of 45 O.R.'s (reinforcements) joined from M.G.C. Base Depôt. Casualties NIL	ref
	5th		Sun shone at intervals, visibility good. During the morning Coys carried out tactical exercises with the infantry of their affiliated Brigades. Sports and football took place in the afternoon. During the evening the C.O. entertained all officers in his quarters. Casualties NIL	ref
	6th		Dull, very strong wind, visibility fair. At 01.00 the time was put back to 00.00, thereby changing from Summer to winter Time during the day	ref

Army Form C.2118.

WAR DIARY
or
INTELLIGENCE SUMMARY.
(Erase heading not required.)

Instructions regarding War Diaries and Intelligence Summaries are contained in F.S. Regs., Part II. and the Staff Manual respectively. Title pages will be prepared in manuscript.

Place	Date	Hour	Summary of Events and Information	Remarks and references to Appendices
BEAUVOIS	1st		Fine all day, dull, visibility good, very cold at night. Training was carried out in accordance with APP I. APP I. The afternoon was devoted to sports & recreational training. Casualties NIL.	APP I. c.f.
	2nd		Dull, rain fell intermittently throughout the day, visibility poor. A draft of 2 Offrs & 16 OR's joined from M.G.C. Base Depot. Training was carried out in accordance with APP II. recreational training took place during the afternoon. The C.O. held a Coy commanders conference at 18.30 at B.H.Q. future operations were discussed. Casualties NIL.	APP II c.f.
	3rd		Dull, fine rain fell on several occasions, visibility poor. The day was spent making preparations for moving. Voluntary Church Parade took place. Coys were attached to Brigades as follows C Coy to 125th m.g. Bn., D Coy to 126th m.g. Bn, B Coy to 127th m.g. Bn. and A Coy in divisional reserve. D Coy moved off at 20.15 & marched to billets in SOLESMES. Coy H.Qrs were established at E.2.c.9.4. B Coy moved at 22.00 & marched to billets in VIESLY. Coy H.Qrs were established at D.28.c.3.7. Casualties NIL.	c.f.
	4th		Sun shone all day, visibility good. During the course of the day D Coy moved to billets in BEAUDIGNIES, Coy H.Q. were established at R.32.d.3.6. B Coy moved forward to the vicinity of VERTIGNEUL and established H.Qrs at W.29 c.6.7. C Coy moved off from BEAUVOIS at 14.00 & marched to billets in SOLESMES (E.1.c.55.30.) A Coy carried out training during the morning & spent the remainder of the day preparing to move. Casualties NIL.	c.f.
LE QUESNOY	5th		Rain fell all day, visibility very low. During the day Bn H.Q. & Q.M. stores moved to LE QUESNOY, A Coy also moved to LE QUESNOY. B Coy moved to billets in HERBIGNIES and established H.Qrs at M.29.b.44. C Coy moved from	

(4799) Wt. W12839/M1293 75,000. 1/17. D.D. & L., Ltd. Forms/C.2118/14.

WAR DIARY or INTELLIGENCE SUMMARY

Army Form C. 2118.

Place	Date	Hour	Summary of Events and Information	Remarks and references to Appendices
I.36.d.8.1.	6th (cont)		Casualties NIL	ccf
	7th		Dull, strong winds, visibility poor, heavy rain fell during late afternoon. Coy. trained with infantry of affiliated Brigades during the morning. The afternoon was devoted to preparations for most & forthcoming operations. Casualties NIL	ccf
Q.10.C.1.1.	8th		Rain fell during early morning, sun shone at intervals during remainder of the day, visibility good. Battalion H.Qrs together with Q.M. moved to Q.10.C.1.1. The move was completed at 14.00. C Coy, which was affiliated to 125th Inf Bde moved to R.13.d.5.8, where the Coy remained concentrated. The move was completed at 15.40. D Coy, which was affiliated to 126th Inf Bde moved to, and remained concentrated at R.17.a.5.8. The move was completed by 16.00. B Coy,affiliated to 127th Inf Bde, moved to R.8.C.4.1 and remained concentrated. The move was completed at 15.00. During the course of the morning A Coy, the divisional reserve Coy, moved to, & took over D Coy's camp at Q.9.d.2.0.4. Casualties NIL.	ccf
ESNES	9th		Sun shone all day, visibility good. Battalion H.Qrs. together with Q.M. moved away from Q.10.C.11. at 12.30 and H.Qrs were established at ESNES at 19.00. During the course of the morning A Coy moved forward to M.10.C.5.5. B Coy moved to H.33.c.3.2. The move was completed at 18.00. C Coy moved into billets in ESNES. The move was completed at 17.00. D Coy moved to N.10.C.2.14. The move was completed at 12.45. Casualties NIL	APP II
	10th		Rain fell during the early morning. Sun shone during the remainder of the day, visibility good. A Coy moved up to ESNES during the early morning. The move was completed at 08.30. During the afternoon C Coy moved to I.15.b.0.2. Casualties NIL	ccf
	11th		Rain fell all day, visibility very bad. A Coy moved to BEAUVOIS. The move was completed at 10.30. D Coy moved to FONTAINE-au-PIRE. The	ccf

Army Form C. 2118.

WAR DIARY
or
INTELLIGENCE SUMMARY.
(Erase heading not required.)

Instructions regarding War Diaries and Intelligence Summaries are contained in F. S. Regs., Part II. and the Staff Manual respectively. Title pages will be prepared in manuscript.

Place	Date	Hour	Summary of Events and Information	Remarks and references to Appendices
ESNES	11th (cont)		move was completed at 10.45. C Coy moved forward to the vicinity of AULICOURT FARM. Casualties NIL	ref.
BEAUVOIS	12th		Sun shone in the early morning, rain commenced to fall just before midday & continued for the remainder of the day, visibility very low. Battn H.Q. & Q.M. moved to BEAUVOIS, the move was completed at 10.00. The 42nd Div relieved the New Zealand Division in the Left sector of the Corps front on the night 12/13th. C Coy 42nd Bn M.G.C. and 2 sections of A Coy 42nd Bn M.G.C. relieved the WELLINGTON and AUCKLAND Coys. N.Z. M.G. Battn in the line. The relief was completed at 02.30 on 13-10-18. C Coy H.Qrs were established at J.3.c.25.80. During the afternoon 12-10-18. D Coy moved forward into support in the vicinity of AULICOURT FARM.	
	13th		Our artillery was very active throughout the night. Hostile artillery shelled FONTAINE - AU-TERTE FARM with 5.9" & 4.2" from extreme range. VIESLY was intermittently shelled. Hostile M.Gs fired down roads leading from D.11 & D.16 and fired also on the road in the vicinity of SAND PIT near VIESLY. Casualties NIL. D Coy moved up to BEAUVOIS during the morning into reserve. Hostile artillery showed considerable activity; FONTAINE-AU-TERTE FARM and the areas D.12.a & b were intermittently shelled throughout the period under review. D.16.d. & D.17.C. were heavily shelled with H.E. and Gas (mustard) from 13.00 to 18.30. The enemy counter attacked at 16.15 and retook BELLE VUE. Enemy M.Gs were very active. There was very little aerial activity. Casualties NIL	ref.
	14th		Sun shone until midday, afternoon was dull, visibility good. Night was cold & hazy. Hostile artillery showed normal activity, FONTAINE-AU-TERTE FARM, QUIEVY and VIESLY were intermittently shelled throughout the whole 24 hours. The areas D.21.b & d were lightly shelled. BELLE VUE was shelled at 18.00. Hostile M.Gs were less active than usual. There was very considerable aerial activity on both sides.	ref.

WAR DIARY or INTELLIGENCE SUMMARY

Army Form C. 2118.

Place	Date	Hour	Summary of Events and Information	Remarks and references to Appendices
BEAUVOIS	14th		Casualties wounded 1 O.R. Training was carried out by Coys not in the line.	ccf.
	15th		Very misty early, fine rain fell during morning, dull during afternoon, visibility very low. Hostile artillery was very active. FONTAINE FARM, BRIASTRE, VIESLY and QUIEVY were shelled at intervals during the day & night with 5.9's, 4.2's and gas shells. Enemy M.Gs fired during the night from the direction of SOLESMES. Our M.Gs fired 12,600 rounds harassing fire during the night onto enemy positions from E.13.6.20 to E.19.6.8.9. Casualties wounded 2 O.R. Training was carried out by Coys not in the line.	ccf.
	16th		Rain fell intermittently all day, visibility very low. The C.O. held a Coy Commanders conference at 13.30. Forthcoming operations were discussed. Hostile artillery showed normal activity, the usual area and villages were intermittently shelled. At 08.00 50 gas shells were dropped in VIESLY. Enemy M.G. carried out harassing fire during the night in D.17.c. Our M.Gs fired 6500 rounds during the night from positions in D.23.a. onto E.13 central & E.19 to 9.9. There was very little aerial activity. Work and several shelters were constructed for gun teams & S.A.A. Casualties NIL. Training was carried out by Coys not in the line.	ccf.
	17th		Dull & overcast, fine rain fell during afternoon, visibility low, very misty at night. Hostile artillery showed normal activity by day and increased activity by night. The usual areas & villages were intermittently shelled throughout the hours under review. Our gun positions in D.22.d. were mainly shelled with H.E. & gas shells at 21.15. Enemy M.Gs carried out harassing fire during the night. Our M.G. fired 8000 rounds harassing fire onto the Railway through in E.7. Several new positions were dug & shelters constructed. The C.O. held a Coy Commanders conference at 17.30 to discuss forthcoming operations. Training was carried out by Coys not in the line. Casualties NIL.	ccf.
	18th		Very misty early, sun shone later, visibility fair. Hostile artillery displayed considerable activity, the usual villages & areas were intermittently shelled. VIESLY was mainly shelled with gas. The back areas were shelled by H.V. guns. Our artillery was very active, harassing the enemy forward & back areas and carrying out a great deal of counter-battery shooting.	ccf.

Army Form C. 2118.

WAR DIARY
or
INTELLIGENCE SUMMARY.
(Erase heading not required)

Place	Date	Hour	Summary of Events and Information	Remarks and references to Appendices
BEAUVOIS	18th (cont)		Sites were dug & camouflaged for guns of C Coy and AUCKLAND COY N.Z. M.G. Batln. for use in forth coming operations. The C.O. held a Coy Commanders Conference at 17.30 at B.H.Q. The final arrangements for the coming attack were discussed. Casualties Wounded Ors 12 O.R.	ref
	19th		Dull, fine rain fell intermittently throughout the day. Visibility very low. During the afternoon & evening A Coy moved forward by stages to assembly position West of the SELLE RIVER in D.18.c. A Coy was affiliated to the 125th Inf Bde. & C Coy same - into Divisional Reserve. AUCKLAND COY N.Z. M.G. Batln. moved up during the early evening to assembly position in the vicinity of D.17.a.+c. 1 Section of C Coy moved to site in D.17.c. D Coy (affiliated to 126th Inf Bde) moved to assembly positions West of the SELLE RIVER in D.18.c during the evening. The situation on the Divisional front was normal all day. Hostile artillery + M.G. employed was actively. Casualties Wounded ORs 5 O.R.	ref
	20th		Very dull, fine rain fell throughout the day, visibility was very low. At 02.00 the 42nd Division renewed the offensive. 2 Sections of C Coy and AUCKLAND COY N.Z. M.G. Batln. provided covering fire for the attack by the 125th Inf Bde. 90,000 rounds were fired. At 08.30 C Coy moved back to billets in BEAUVOIS and AUCKLAND COY rejoined the N.Z. M.G. Batln. A + D Coys crossed the SELLE RIVER with pack animals shortly after ZERO and took up positions on the high ground in the vicinity of the GREEN LINE and hostile patrols & infantry digging in were engaged with considerable effect. Coy H Qrs of both companies were established in the railway cutting at E.13.c.8.4. A + D Coys supplied covering fire for the attack of the 127th Inf Bde, which was pressed through the 126th Inf Bde on the GREEN LINE, moving to the Division on the right flank failing to take the high ground in E.15.d. + E.21.a. This attack was not entirely successful. A + D Coys fired 57,000 rounds covering this attack. At 0100 B Coy (affiliated to 127th Inf Bde) moved up from BEAUVOIS and crossed the SELLE RIVER with animals, it was found impossible to get sunken across the railway, so loads were transferred to pack animals. Before this proved forward with a view of consolidating the BROWN LINE, but no information was received that the BROWN LINE had not been taken and that the enemy	

(A7099) Wt. W12850/M1293. 75,000. 1/17. D.D. & L., Ltd. Forms/C.2118/14.

WAR DIARY or INTELLIGENCE SUMMARY

Army Form C. 2118.

Place	Date	Hour	Summary of Events and Information	Remarks and references to Appendices
BEAUVOIS	20th (cont)		were hild up. B Coy therefore consolidated the line along the road in E.8.c, E.14.b & E.15.c with one section covering the left flank as touch had not been gained with the left division & the situation was obscure. At 13.00 A Coy took up their positions with a view to protecting the right flank and obtaining depth in depth. Sections took up the following positions, E.14.a.5.2, E.20.a.2.4., E.19.b.9.2., and D.24.a.8.7. C Coy H.Qrs. were moved to D.24.a.8.7. During the afternoon D Coy consolidated the GREEN LINE. At 16.00 the division on the right methilized & gained the high ground in E.15.d & E.22.a. The 127th and 8ns conforming. During the night B Coy consolidated the BROWN LINE with guns in the following positions, 2 guns at E.3.b.7.5. E.3.b.9.9.40, E.9.c.8.9, E.9.d.3.9, E.9.d.3.8 and 1 Section at E.9.d.3.6. B Coys H.Qrs. were established at E.13.c.8.4. No objectives, times & particulars of covering fire are trace. Throughout the day hostile artillery & M.Gs. displayed great activity. The whole area was considerably shelled. Casualties. Killed LIEUT. G. F. ASHTON. M.G.C. and 3.O.R. Wounded 33 O.R. Wounded at duty 2 O.R. Dull, visibility very poor early in the day, sun shone later when visibility improved considerably. At 11.00 C Coy was attached to 125th and 8n and moved up to the line staying at GUISETTE FARM and during the evening relieved B Coy. The relief was completed at 23.00. B Coy on being moved to billets at HERPIGNY FARM arriving at approx 03.00 on 21-10-18. A Coy came into divisional reserve and during the course of the day moved back to billets in BEAUVOIS. Hostile artillery was very active, the railway in E.13 & 19, BRIASTRE, BELLE VUE and the forward areas received particular attention. There was considerable aerial activity. Roads in the back areas were harassed by hostile H.V. guns. Casualties Killed 2 O.R. Wounded 10 O.R.	APP III CCR
	21st		Dull, fine from till at intervals throughout the day, visibility poor During the course of the afternoon B Coy moved from its billets at BEAUVOIS. Two sections of D Coy went to withdrawn to billets at AULCOURT FARM during the evening. Hostile artillery was still very active, particularly against the railway in E.13 & 19, BRIASTRE was intermittently shelled	CCR

Conrad? Pa N 1b
(A 7991) Wt. W12893/M12303 75,000. 1/17. D.D. & L., Ltd. Forms/C.2118/4.

WAR DIARY or INTELLIGENCE SUMMARY

Army Form C. 2118.

Place	Date	Hour	Summary of Events and Information	Remarks and references to Appendices
BEAUVOIS	23rd		Fine, sun shone all day, visibility good. Preparations to the attack by the 125F arty Bde at 03.26. The guns of C Coy and two sections of D Coy were withdrawn at 02.15 to assembly positions in sunken Roads E.9.d.1, E.3.6 & D and MAROU where they remained during the initial barrage. Sections moved forward behind advancing battalions and reached the following positions at 07.00, 4 guns C Coy at E.4.C, 6 guns C Coy at W.28.c, and 8 guns D Coy at W.28.c.7.8 at 08.40. Fire was opened to cover the advance of the 2nd N.Z. Brigade, onto the following targets - W.30.a central, cross Roads W.24.a.11, W.24.c central, E.10 central + W.23.a.9.9. Fire was continued as long as observance permitted. A large party of enemy was engaged at W.24.c.0.7 and many casualties were inflicted. During the operation 65,000 rounds were fired. Later in the day C Coy moved near to VIESLY into billets. 2 Sections of D Coy moved from AVESNES COURT FARM to BEAUVOIS reaching the latter place at 13.00. The 2 sections of D Coy in the line moved back during the course of the day & rejoined the Coy at BEAUVOIS at 15.00. A draft of 15 O.Rs joined from M.G.C. Base Depot. The Coys at BEAUVOIS spent the day resting & cleaning up. Casualties NIL	C.O.R.
	24th		Fine, sunny, visibility good. C Coy moved back to billets in BEAUVOIS, arriving at 14.00. The day was devoted to resting & cleaning up & overhauling guns & equipment. Recreational training took place during the afternoon. A draft of 17 O.Rs joined from M.G.C. Base Depot. Casualties NIL	C.O.R.
	25th		Fine but dull, visibility fair. A draft of 10 O.Rs joined from M.G.C. Base Depot. The C.O. held a Coy Commanders conference at 12.00. The distance covered during the last operation went into ⟨?⟩. The day was devoted to bathing & overhauling equipment & recreational training. Casualties NIL	C.O.R.

Army Form C. 2118.

WAR DIARY
or
INTELLIGENCE SUMMARY.
(Erase heading not required.)

Instructions regarding War Diaries and Intelligence Summaries are contained in F. S. Regs., Part II. and the Staff Manual respectively. Title pages will be prepared in manuscript.

Place	Date	Hour	Summary of Events and Information	Remarks and references to Appendices
BEAUVOIS	26th		Sun shone at intervals throughout the day, visibility good. The C.O. inspected 'A' Coy at 10.00, 'B' Coy at 11.00 & 'D' Coy at 12.00. The afternoon was devoted to football & other sports. During the morning the C.O. lectured all officers and N.C.O's. A draft of 1 officer + 47 O.Rs joined from M.G.C. Base Depôt. Casualties NIL	cert.
	27th		Sun shone during the early morning. Fine rain fell at intervals later. Visibility fair. During the morning the battalion was inspected by the Divisional commander and a presentation of medal ribbon took place. Football was played in the afternoon. Casualties NIL	cert.
	28th		Sun shone all day, visibility good. During the morning all four companies passed through the gas chamber, and general training was carried out. The afternoon was spent playing football. Casualties NIL	cert.
	29th		Sun shone all day, visibility very good. Coys carried out the following training during the morning. Range work, P.T., Laying gun by compass, squad drill & elementary gun work. The afternoon was devoted to recreational training. Casualties NIL	cert.
	30th		Sun, sun shone all day, strong wind, visibility good, cold at night. Coys carried out training in accordance with APP IV Casualties NIL	APP IV cert.
	31st		Fine rain fell during early morning, fine later, visibility poor. Training was carried out in accordance with APP V Casualties NIL	APP V

M. H. Tillie
Lieut. Col.
Comdg. 42nd Battn M.G.C.

APP I

42nd. BATTALION, M.G.C.
TRAINING PROGRAMME FOR
THURSDAY, OCTOBER 3rd. 1918.

9.00 to 13.00.   Inspection of Companies by Commanding Officer.
                 Instruction in First Aid and 1 hours P.T.
                 Cleaning of Guns and Stores. Replacing of
                 ammunition in belts etc.

14.00.   Recreational Training.

2.9.18.   CCRose
                                     Capt. & Adjt.,
                              for O.C. 42nd. Battalion, M.G.C.

APP II

SECRET.

Copy No. 5

42nd. BATTALION, M.G.C. ORDER NO. 29.

October 8th. 1918.

"A" Company, 42nd. Battalion, M.G.C. will move tomorrow to the vicinity of M.10.b.central.

The present camp will be cleared by 7.50a.m.

Lieut.-Colonel,
Cmdg. 42nd. Battalion, M.G.C.

Distribution.
Copy No. 1. "A" Coy.
" "   2. 42nd. Divn. 'Q'
" "   3. Signalling Officer.
" "   4 & 5. War Diary.
" "   6. File.

APP II

O.C. A. Company.
" B. "
" C. "
" D. "

42nd. Division 'G'

1. In the event of an enemy attack the following Companies will move forward and occupy positions as on attached map.

2. The Companies will move with fighting limbers only in battle order.

3. The role of the Division is:-
   (i). To counter-attack.
   (ii). To hold the PURPLE and RED LINES.

4. The role of M.Gs. is:-
   (i). To form a skeleton of defence at the onset.
   (ii). To be subsequently prepared to co-operate in counter-attacks on BEER TRENCH as previously outlined.
   (iii). To co-operate in holding the PURPLE and RED LINES.

5. A reserve of 4,000 rounds of S.A.A. will be held at every gun position and 20,000 at H.Qrs. of D. A. and C. Companies.

6. O.C. Companies will arrange to keep sufficient limbers to give mobility for counter-attack in covered positions until the situation is clear and definite information is received.

7. **Dispositions.**

"D" Company.
H.Qrs. J.5.d.9.2.
2 guns K.1.a.2.6.
2 " K.1.c.5.6.
2 " K.7.c.0.7.
2 " K.13.a.5.3.
2 " K.13.a.2.0.
2 " J.24.a.9.8.
2 " J.5.d.9.3.
2 " J.11.b.7.7.

"A" Company.
H.Qrs. J.5.c.6.4.
2 guns J.5.b.0.1.
2 " J.3.d.1.8.
2 " J.11.a.3.3.
2 " J.10.d.2.7.
2 " J.9.d.3.5.
2 " J.9.b.5.7.
2 " J.4.a.9.2.
2 " J.4.a.4.9.

"C" Company.
H.Qrs. D.17.a.7.5.
2 guns E.19.a.0.1.
2 " E.19.c.1.9.
2 " D.24.c.0.2.
2 " D.2X.d.0.1.
2 " D.20.a.2.9.
2 " D.26.c.5.3.
5 " D.19.a.4.2.
1 " D.19.a.3.4.

8. **Action of Reserve.** O.C. 'B' Company will move Company in Battle Order to position of assembly in D.19.d. establishing his H.Qrs. near Battn. Visual Station at D.25.b.7.3.
He will park at 50 yards interval between Sections and await orders in readiness to move at ½ hours notice.
All Officers, N.C.Os. and Scouts will reconnoitre Divisional Front, including counter-attack positions.

9. Battalion Headquarters will be at D.26.d.4.0. Companies will report when in position.

Lieut-Colonel,
O.C. 42nd. Battalion, M.G.Corps.

6.6.18.

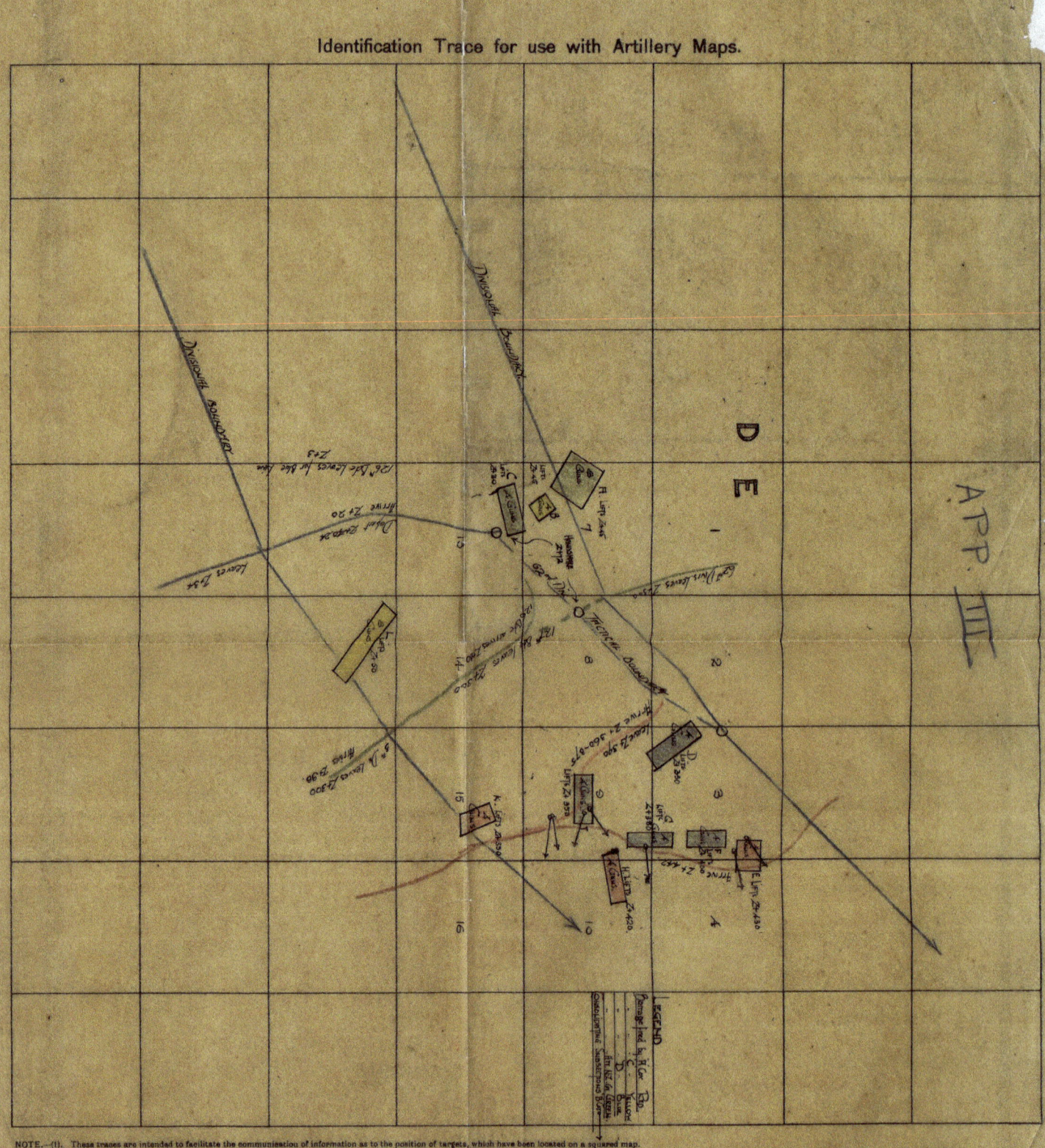

42nd. BATTALION, M.G. CORPS.
TRAINING PROGRAMME FOR WEDNESDAY, OCTR. 30th. 1918.

"A" Company.	"B" Company.	"C" Company.	"D" Company.
08.45. Coy. Parade.	08.45. Coy. Parade.	08.45. Coy. Parade.	08.45. Coy. Parade.
09.00 - 13.00. % P.T. % Combined Drill. % Range Work.	09.00 - 09.45. Squad Drill. Handling of Arms.	09.00 - 10.00. Squad Drill & P.T.	09.00 - 09.45. Squad Drill.
	10.00 - 13.00. Section Tactical Exercises.	10.15 - 11.15. Laying out Lines of Fire by Compass.	10.00 - 10.45. P.T.
Afternoon. Recreational Training.		11.30 - 13.00. % Range work.	11.00 - 13.00. Section Tactical Exercises.
	Afternoon. Recreational Training.	Afternoon. Recreational Training.	Afternoon. Recreational Training.

All the above training will be carried out in the vicinity of billets at BEAUVOIS except training marked % which will be carried out at I.4.c.7.3.

TP.1.
29.10.18.

ccRose Capt. for O.C.
42nd. Battalion, M.G.C.

989

Confidential
(Original.)

War Diary
of
42nd Battalion Machine Gun Corps

Volume IX

From 1-11-18   To 30-11-18

WAR DIARY
or
INTELLIGENCE SUMMARY.
(Erase heading not required.)

Army Form C. 2118.

Place	Date	Hour	Summary of Events and Information	Remarks and references to Appendices
LE QUESNOY	5ᵗʰ	(cont)	SOLESMES to WILLIES in BEAUDIGNIES. During the night the 4/2ⁿᵈ Div. relieved the N.Z. Div. in the line. D Coy relieved guns of the N.Z. M.G. Battn. in the following positions:- 4 guns at O.22.c.5.0., 2 guns in O.20.b., 1 gun at O.19.d.9.0., 1 gun at N.24.a.6.2. Coy H.Qrs. T & S gun in reserve at N.24.a.6.3. Rear Coy H.Qrs. were established at N.20.c.9.7. During the relief, owing to the roads being blown, pack animals were used to get the guns forward. Counting was very slow & consequently casualties to M.Gs. Casualties Killed. Pvate W.C. Taylor (M.G.C). Wounded 2 O.Rs. Rain fell during the whole period under review. Visibility very low.	cont
M.36.d.1.7.	6ᵗʰ		During the early morning B Coy moved from HERBIGNIES and became temporarily attached to the 12ᵗʰ & 14ᵗʰ Bdes. to defend the Right flank of the Division. The following positions were taken up:- 4 guns in O.15.d., 12 guns T Coy H.Qrs at N.24.a.9.6. At 12.30 the Division on our immediate Right advanced & the guns in O.15.d. were withdrawn to positions in O.20.b. During the course of the day Battn. H.Qrs. moved to M.36.d.1.7. and Q.M. Stores moved to LE CARNOY. C. Coy. moved forward to WILLIES in HERBIGNIES and A Coy moved to LE CARNOY. Casualties NIL. Rain fell intermittently during the whole 24 hours. Visibility very low.	cont
	7ᵗʰ		During the morning 2 Sections of D Coy worked forward with the infantry, 1 section being attached to 1/9ᵗʰ Manchesters & the other to 1/10ᵗʰ Manchesters. A reserve section of D Coy moved up to the FARM de la FOSSE and two guns advanced with the infantry crossing the river at P.23.c.4.4. and coming into action from the first floor of a house in P.23.d.9.4. engaged & effectively silenced a hostile battery of 77 m.m. guns in Q.20.c. D Coy H Qrs went moved forward to O.22.c.5.6. & near H Qrs moved to FORESTERS HOUSE NORTH. C. Coy moved forward to HARGNIES. Casualties NIL.	cont

Army Form C. 2118.

WAR DIARY
or
INTELLIGENCE SUMMARY.
(Erase heading not required.)

Place	Date	Hour	Summary of Events and Information	Remarks and references to Appendices
HARGNIES	8.F.		Rain fell intermittently during the day; visibility very low. Snow at night. During the morning the 125th and Bde. passed through the 126th and Bde. and sections of D Coy were temporarily attached to 1/5th, 1/17th and 1/8th L.F. The section attached to 1/5th L.F. advanced to P.29.d where they consolidated. The section attached to 1/5th L.F. advanced with the leading supporting coy using fighting sections to V.H.a.3.9 from which point the guns were man-handled to positions in P.35.b commanding the ground East of HAUTMONT and the high ground in Q.31. The third section with 1/8th L.F. remained in support. Batln. H.Qrs. & Q.M. Stores moved to HARGNIES. A Coy. moved to BOUSSIERES staying at HARGNIES & became attached to Ox.125th and Bde. C Coy, which was already attached to 125th and Bde, moved forward into position with two sections covering the Right flank from P.33.c. The remaining two sections were held in reserve in BOUSSIERES. Coy H.Qrs. were established at P.32.a.7.7. B Coy rejoined the 127th and Bde & moved to HARGNIES where B coy came into Divisional Reserve. D Coy's H.Qrs. were moved to Q.0.24.6.9 during the evening. Casualties: Wounded 2 O.Rs.	cof.
	9.		Sun shone all day. Visibility very good. Heavy frost at night. At dawn A Coy took over from D Coy, D Coy on relief proceeded to VIEUX MESNIL. By dusk C Coys guns covering the Right flank were withdrawn and the final objective was consolidated with sections in Q.35.b, Q.31.a, Q.20.a and 1 section in reserve at Coy H.Qrs at P.29.c.8.8. A Coy conformed, supporting C Coy, with sections distributed in P.35.b, P.32.a, P.23.d and 1 section in reserve at Coy H.Qrs at P.29.c.8.8. Casualties NIL.	cof.
HAUTMONT	10.F.		Sun shone all day, visibility very good. During the morning Batln. H.Qrs. & Q.M. Stores moved to HAUTMONT. D Coy moved to billets in HAUTMONT.	

(2708) Wt. W18859/M1293-750,000. 1/17. D. D. & L., Ltd. Forms/C.2118/44.

Army Form C. 2118.

WAR DIARY
or
INTELLIGENCE SUMMARY.
(Erase heading not required.)

Instructions regarding War Diaries and Intelligence Summaries are contained in F. S. Regs., Part II. and the Staff Manual respectively. Title pages will be prepared in manuscript.

Place	Date	Hour	Summary of Events and Information	Remarks and references to Appendices
HAUTMONT	10th	(cont)	During the afternoon A Coy took over the defence of the 5th Divisional Front with sections at W.3.c.9.1. Q.33.c.8.2, Q.31.a.1.5 & FONTAINE. Casualties NIL	ccf
	11th		Sun but dull, cold, visibility bad. Rain fell during the evening. Bostilities ceased at 11.00. During the afternoon the sections of A & C Coys were withdrawn to billets in HAUTMONT. Casualties NIL	ccf
	12th		Sun shone all day, visibility good, cold. B Coy moved to HAUTMONT during the morning. The day was devoted to cleaning up & overhauling guns & equipment. Recreational training took place during the afternoon. The C.O. held a Coy Commanders conference at 17.00 at B.H.Q. future arrangements were discussed. Casualties NIL	ccf
	13th		The Coys came under the orders of the C.O. Dull, cold, sunny all day, visibility good. Cleaning up & overhauling of guns & equipment was continued. Games & sports took place during the afternoon. A composite party from the battalion took part in a memorial service. Casualties Nil.	ccf
	14th		Sun shone all day, visibility excellent, very cold. Route march, Bathing & recreational training took place.	ccf
	15th		Cold, sunny, visibility excellent. M.G. Training, Physical Training & Squad Drill were carried out during the morning. The afternoon was devoted to recreational training. During the morning a composite Coy took part in the rehearsal of the presentation of guns to the MAIRE of HAUTMONT.	ccf
	16th		Sun shone all day, visibility very good. Training was carried out in accordance with APP III	APP III

Army Form C. 2118.

WAR DIARY
or
INTELLIGENCE SUMMARY.
(Erase heading not required.)

Instructions regarding War Diaries and Intelligence Summaries are contained in F.S. Regs., Part II. and the Staff Manual respectively. Title pages will be prepared in manuscript.

Place	Date	Hour	Summary of Events and Information	Remarks and references to Appendices
HAUTMONT	16th (cont)		A composite Coy took part in the presentation of captured guns to the mayor.	ccf
	17th		Dull, very cold, visibility low. Voluntary Church Parade took place. 70 O.Rs attended a lecture by the G.H.Q. Demobilization officer. A draft of 3 O.Rs joined from M.G.C. Base Depot.	ccf
	18th		Cold, snow & rain fell during the afternoon, visibility low. Training was carried out in accordance with APP III. The C.O. held a conference at 15.00 at B.H.Q. Coy Commanders & Seconds in command attended. The principal subjects discussed were (1) The importance of not "slacking off" (2) Sports & recreation.	APP III ccf
	19th		Dull, rain fell at intervals, visibility very low. Training was carried out in accordance with APP V	APP V ccf
	20th		Sun shone at intervals, heavy mist during the afternoon. Training was carried out in accordance with APP VI	APP VI ccf
	21st		Fine, cold, sun shone at intervals, visibility very low. Training was carried out in accordance with APP VII	APP VII ccf
	22nd		Sun shone all day, heavy frost at night. Training was carried out in accordance with APP VIII.	APP VIII ccf
	23rd		Sunny all day, mild. Training was carried out in accordance with APP IX. A draft of 32 O.Rs joined from M.G.C Base Depot. The C.O. held a Coy Commanders conference at 17.30 hours at B.H.Q.	APP IX ccf
	24th		Fine but dull, cold. Voluntary Church Parade took place. Recreational training took place during the afternoon.	ccf

(A7598. Wt. W2899/M1793. 1/17. D.D. & L. Ltd. Forms/C2118/4)

Army Form C. 2118.

WAR DIARY
or
INTELLIGENCE SUMMARY.
(Erase heading not required.)

Instructions regarding War Diaries and Intelligence Summaries are contained in F. S. Regs., Part II. and the Staff Manual respectively. Title pages will be prepared in manuscript.

Place	Date	Hour	Summary of Events and Information	Remarks and references to Appendices
HAUTMONT	25th		Rain fell intermittently throughout the day. Training was carried out in accordance with APP X	APP X car
"	26th		Dull, fine, visibility very low. Training was carried out in accordance with APP XI	APP XI cur
"	27th		Dull, fine rain fell during the night. Training was carried out in accordance with APP XII	APP XII cur
"	28th		Fine rain fell at intervals throughout the day. Training was carried out in accordance with APP XII	APP XIII car
"	29th		Fine all day, dull, spots of rain. Training was carried out in accordance with APP XIV	APP XIV cler
"	30th		Dull, cold, windy. Training was carried out in accordance with APP XV	APP XV cur

W. K. Gillie
Lieut Col.
Cmg 42nd Battn. M.G.C.

Vol 10

Confidential
(Original)

WAR DIARY
of
42nd Battalion M.G. Corps.

Volume X

From 1-12-18   To 31-12-18.

Army Form C. 2118.

WAR DIARY
or
INTELLIGENCE SUMMARY.
(Erase heading not required.)

Instructions regarding War Diaries and Intelligence Summaries are contained in F.S. Regs., Part II. and the Staff Manual respectively. Title pages will be prepared in manuscript.

Place	Date	Hour	Summary of Events and Information	Remarks and references to Appendices
HAUTMONT	1st		Fine, very cold, sunny.	ccf
	2nd		During the morning His majesty the King visited the Divisional area. The Battalion lined a portion of the AVESNES - MAUBEUGE Road. Voluntary Church Parades took place during the day. The afternoon was devoted to Recreational Training.	APP I ccf
	3rd		Full but fine, cold wind. Training was carried out in accordance with APP II	APP II ccf
	4th		Dull, fine rain fell all day. Training was carried out in accordance with APP II. A draft of 27 O.R. (Reinforcements) joined from M.G.C. Base Depot.	APP III ccf
	5th		Fine rain fell all day. Training was carried out in accordance with APP III.	APP IV ccf
	6th		Fine, sun shone at intervals. Training was carried out in accordance with APP IV.	APP V ccf
	7th		Fine, sun shone all day. Training was carried out in accordance with APP V.	APP VI ccf
	8th		Dull, wet, misty. Training was carried out in accordance with APP VI. Sun shone all day, visibility excellent. Voluntary Church Parade took place during the morning. The afternoon was devoted to Recreational Training.	
	9th		Dull rain fell at intervals throughout the day.	ccf

(A7092). Wt. W12839/AC593. 75,000. 1/17. D.D. & L., Ltd. Forms/C2118/4.

Army Form C. 2118.

WAR DIARY
or
INTELLIGENCE SUMMARY.
(Erase heading not required.)

Instructions regarding War Diaries and Intelligence Summaries are contained in F. S. Regs., Part II. and the Staff Manual respectively. Title pages will be prepared in manuscript.

Place	Date	Hour	Summary of Events and Information	Remarks and references to Appendices
HAUTMONT	9th (cont)		Training was carried out in accordance with APP VII	APP VII cont.
	10th		Rain fell during the day, cold.	APP VIII cont.
	11th		Training was carried out in accordance with APP VIII	
			Rainy cold, fine during afternoon.	
	12th		Training was carried out in accordance with APP IX	APP IX cont.
			Rain fell all day, strong wind.	
	13th		Training was carried out in accordance with APP X	APP X cont.
			Rainy early, sun shone during afternoon.	
	14th		The day was spent preparing for the move	cont.
			Rain fell early, sunny during afternoon.	
ROCQ	14th		The battalion moved to billets in ROCQ. The move was completed at 13.00	cont.
			Fine, dull	
BONNE ESPERANCE	15th		The battalion moved to billets in BONNE ESPERANCE. The move was completed at 15.00	cont.
			Rain fell during the morning, fine later, strong wind	
LEERNES	16th		The battalion moved to billets in LEERNES. The move was completed at 14.15	cont.
	17th		Rain fell at intervals all day	cont.
			The day was spent clearing up + resting	
			Heavy rain fell all day, strong wind, cold.	
MARCHIENNE AU PONT	18th		The battalion moved to billets in MARCHIENNE-AU-PONT. The move was completed at 11.35	cont.
			Rain fell during early morning + evening. Fine remainder of day, sun shone at intervals. Cold wind	
VELAINE	19th		The battalion moved to billets in VELAINE and KEUMIÉE. The move was completed at 14.30	cont.
	20th		Heavy rain fell at intervals	

WAR DIARY
or
INTELLIGENCE SUMMARY.
(Erase heading not required.)

Army Form C. 2118.

Instructions regarding War Diaries and Intelligence Summaries are contained in F. S. Regs., Part II. and the Staff Manual respectively. Title pages will be prepared in manuscript.

Place	Date	Hour	Summary of Events and Information	Remarks and references to Appendices
VELAINE	20th (cont)		This day was devoted to cleaning up.	cef.
	21st		Sun all day, cold.	cef.
			The day was spent cleaning up & readjusting units. Recreational Training took place in the afternoon.	
	22nd		Sun, cold. Very slight shower during afternoon.	cef.
			20 O.R's N.C.O's & Privates were sent to Demobilization concentration camp. Games were played during the afternoon. The C.O. held a Coy Commanders conference at B.H.Q. at 10.30. A draft of 3 offrs joined from M.G.C Base Depot. Sleet fell throughout the day.	
	23rd		Very strong wind, heavy rain + sleet fell throughout the day.	cef.
			23 O.R's N.C.O's, Privates & Bang service men were sent to Demob. concentration camp	
	24th		Sun all day, snow fell at night	cef.
			Bathing took place in the morning. 15 O.R's went to Demob. Con. Camp. A draft of 1 offr and 44 O.R's joined from M.G.C Base Depot	
	25th		Sun shone all day, cold.	cef.
			The Divisional Commander inspected the unit dressed in drawing hall during the morning. 9 O.R's proceeded to Demob. Con. Camp.	
	26th		Sun shining, cold.	cef.
			2 O.R's proceeded to Demob. Con. Camp.	
	27th		Rain fell all day, strong wind.	cef.
			The day was devoted to Xmas festivities. The Bn. Band played during the afternoon.	
	28th		Strong wind, rain fell all day. A lecture was given by Mr Purdom at 17.00 in the drawing Proston.	cef.
	29th		Very strong wind, heavy rain fell all day.	cef.

WAR DIARY
or
INTELLIGENCE SUMMARY.
(Erase heading not required.)

Army Form C. 2118.

Place	Date	Hour	Summary of Events and Information	Remarks and references to Appendices
VELAINE	29th (cont)		Voluntary Church Parade took place during the morning. Windy, showery, mild. Oat Coys football.	ref
	30th		The C.O. gave a lecture at 12.00 to all Officers & N.C.Os. on Routine matters etc., but fine rain fell during the afternoon	ref
	31st		The Divisional Band played during the morning & afternoon	ref

W.A.Tite .... Lieut Col.
Commanding 42nd Bn M.G.C.

APP I

42nd. BATTALION, N.G.C.
TRAINING PROGRAMME FOR MONDAY, DECEMBER 2nd. 1918.

MORNING.   All Companies Route March.

Route.   BAUTMONT – cross roads at P.30.b.4.3. – LES GRAVETTES –
FERNIER la GRANDE – cross roads at Q.23.c.5.5. –
LE CAMP LE LOUP – MANIERE – BEAUFORT – cross roads at
W.1.b.7.3. – road junction at W.1.b.4.1. – road junction
at Q.5I.b.9.4. – HAUTMONT.

Companies will be inspected in the Square at 10.00 hours
by the Commanding Officer prior to moving off.

AFTERNOON.   RECREATIONAL TRAINING.

                                              Ross
                                        Capt. for O.C.,
1.12.18.   42nd. Battalion, N.G.C.

APP II

42nd. BATTALION, M.G.C.
TRAINING PROGRAMME FOR TUESDAY, DECEMBER 3rd. 1918.

'A' Company.	'B' Company.	'C' Company.	'D' Company.
0900. Coy. Parade.	0900. Coy. Parade.	0900 – 1030. Baths.	0900. Coy. Parade.
0915 – 1000. Squad Drill Handling of Arms.	0915 – 1015. Squad & Arms Drill.	1100 – 1130. Lecture "Demobilization Procedure".	0915 – 1015. Cleaning Guns & Equipment.
1000 – 1100. Lecture "Interior Economy".	1030 – 1115. Practice Packing of Limbers.	1130 – 1230. P.T.	1030 – 1200. Baths.
1100 – 1200. P.T.	1130 – 1230. P.T.	P.T. on Football Field (P.24.a.8.2.) Remainder in vicinity of Billets.	All training in vicinity of Billets.
Squad Drill & P.T. on Football Field (P.25.b.2.1.) Remainder in vicinity of Billets.	Squad Drill & P.T. in grounds of Chateau du Clos.		

AFTERNOON. 'A' and 'B' Company. – Baths.
All Companies. – Recreational Training.

ce Rose
Capt. for O.C.,
42nd. Battalion, M.G.Corps.

2.12.18.

APP III

42nd. BATTALION, M.G.C.
TRAINING PROGRAMME FOR WEDNESDAY, DECEMBER 4th. 1918.

"A" Company.	"B" Company.	"C" Company.	"D" Company.
0900. Coy. Parade.	0900. Coy. Parade.	0900. Coy. Parade.	0900 - 1000. Coy. Parade. Inspection of Kit.
0915 - 1000. Squad Drill. Handling of Arms.	0920 - 1020. Squad Drill. Handling of Arms.	0915 - 1100. Cleaning Guns & Equipment.	1015 - 1100. Company Drill.
1000 - 1100. Cleaning Guns & Equipment.	1035 - 1130. Lecture "Interior Economy."	1100 - 1145. P.T.	1115 - 1200. Cleaning and Refilling Belts.
1100 - 1200. P.T.	1145 - 1230. P.T.	1145 - 1230. Squad Drill.	1200 - 1230. Lecture "Discipline".
1200 - 1300. Musketry.	Squad Drill & P.T. in grounds of Chateau du Ulea. Remainder in vicinity of Billets.	Squad Drill & P.T. on Football Field (P.24.a.8.2.) Remainder in vicinity of Billets.	Coy. Drill on Football Field. (P.23.d.5.9.) Remainder in vicinity of Billets.
Squad Drill, P.T. & Musketry on Football Field (P.23.b.2.1.) Remainder in vicinity of Billets.			

AFTERNOON — RECREATIONAL TRAINING.

3.12.18.   CC Ross   Capt. for O.C., 42nd. Bn. M.G.C.

APP IV

42nd. BATTALION, M.G.C.
TRAINING PROGRAMME FOR THURSDAY, DECEMBER 5th. 1918.

'A' Company.	'B' Company.	'C' Company.	'D' Company.
0900. Coy. Parade.	0900. Coy. Parade.	0900. Coy. Parade.	0900. Coy. Parade.
0925 – 1000. Squad Drill. Handling of A.	0900 – 1000. Squad Drill. Handling of A.	0915 – 1100. Cleaning Guns & Equipment.	0915 – 1000. Gun Drill.
1000 – 1100. P.T.	1015 – 1115. Cleaning Guns & Equipment.	1100 – 1145. P.T.	1015 – 1100. Immediate Action.
1100 – 1300. Kit Inspection.	1130 – 1230. P.T.	1145 – 1230. Squad Drill.	1115. Lecture "Interior Economy".
Squad Drill & P.T. on Football Ground(P.23.b.2.1) Remainder in vicinity of Billets.	Squad Drill & P.T. in grounds of Chateau du Clos. Remainder in vicinity of Billets.	Squad Drill & P.T. on Football Field(P.24.a.8.2) Remainder in vicinity of Billets.	Gun Drill and I.A. on Football Field(P.23.d.5.9.) Remainder in vicinity of Billets.

AFTERNOON   =   RECREATIONAL TRAINING.

Capt. for O.C.,
42nd. Battalion, M.G.C.

4.12.18.

APP V

42nd. BATTALION, M.G.C.
TRAINING PROGRAMME FOR FRIDAY, DECEMBER 6th. 1918.

MORNING.   All Companies - Route March.

    Route.   HAUTMONT - along road through P.24.a. & b., to road junction at Q.9.c.1.7. - cross roads at Q.17.c.5.3. - FERRIERE LA GRANDE - LES GRAVETTES - HAUTMONT.

    Companies will be inspected in the Square at 1000 hours by the Commanding Officer, prior to moving off.

AFTERNOON.   Recreational Training.

5.12.18.

                                              Capt. for O.C.,
                                   42nd. Battalion, M.G.Corps.

APP VI

42nd. BATTALION, M.G.C.

TRAINING PROGRAMME FOR SATURDAY, DECEMBER 7th. 1918.

'A' Company.	'B' Company.	'C' Company.	'D' Company.
0900. Coy. Parade.	0900. Coy. Parade.	0900. Coy. Parade.	0900. Coy. Parade.
0915 - 1000. P.T.	0930 - 1030. P.T.	0900 onwards. Interior Economy.	0900 - 0945. P.T.
1000 - 1045. Squad Drill. Handling of Arms. & Equipment.	1045 - 1115. Cleaning Guns & Equipment.	All work in vicinity of Billets.	1000 onwards. Interior Economy.
1100 - 1200. Cleaning Guns & Equipment.	1130 - 1230. Lecture "Canada"		P.T. on Football Ground (P.23.d.5.9.) Remainder in vicinity of Billets.
1200 - 1300. Kit Inspection.	P.T. in grounds of Chateau in Mos. Remainder in vicinity of Billets.		
Squad Drill & P.T. vicinity of Billets. on Football Ground (P.23.b.8.1.) Remainder in vicinity of Billets.			

AFTERNOON — RECREATIONAL TRAINING.

6.12.18.

Capt. for O.C.,
42nd. Battalion, M.G.C.

APP VII

42nd. BATTALION, M.G.C.
TRAINING PROGRAMME FOR MONDAY, DECEMBER 9th. 1918.

MORNING.   -   All Companies.

                 0900.   Coy. Parade and Inspection.

                 Remainder of Morning.   Interior Economy.

AFTERNOON.   Recreational Training.

8.12.18.

                                       Capt. for O.C.,
                                    42nd. Battalion, M.G. Corps.

APP VIII

42nd. BATTALION, M.G.C.
TRAINING PROGRAMME FOR TUESDAY, DECEMBER 10th. 1918.

MORNING.   All Companies - Route March.

Route.   HAUMONT - cross roads at P.30.b.4.3. - ST. REMY-MAL-BATI -
              road junction at V.10.d.2.3. - road junction at
              V.11.d.1.7. - HAUMONT.

AFTERNOON.   Recreational Training.

9.12.18.   _____ Capt. for O.C.,
                                          42nd. Battalion, M.G.C.

App IX

42nd. BATTALION, M.G.C.
TRAINING PROGRAMME FOR WEDNESDAY, DECEMBER 11th. 1918.

All Companies.

      0900.   Company Parade.

      0900 onwards.   Practice packing for move.

Afternoon.   Recreational Training.

10.12.18.   CC Rose Capt. for O.C.,
                                     42nd. Battalion, M.G.C.

App X

42nd. BATTALION, M.G.C.
TRAINING PROGRAMME FOR THURSDAY, DECEMBER 12th. 1918.

MORNING.   All Companies.

    9a.m.   Coy. Parade.
    9a.m. onwards. Interior Economy.

AFTERNOON.   Recreational Training.

11.12.18.

             Capt. for O.C.,
             42nd. Battalion, M.G.Corps.

Confidential
(original)

WAR DIARY

of

42nd Battalion M.G.C.

From 1-1-19.   To 31-1-19

Volume I

WAR DIARY or INTELLIGENCE SUMMARY

Army Form C. 2118.

(Erase heading not required.)

Instructions regarding War Diaries and Intelligence Summaries are contained in F. S. Regs., Part II. and the Staff Manual respectively. Title pages will be prepared in manuscript.

Place	Date	Hour	Summary of Events and Information	Remarks and references to Appendices
VELAINE	1st		Sun shone at intervals, strong wind.	
			Training was carried out in accordance with APP I. The C.O. held a conference at B.H.Q. at 17.00	APP I c.e.f.
			Coy Commanders & Seconds in command of Coys attended.	
	2nd		A few showers, sunny at intervals, strong wind.	
			Training was carried out in accordance with APP II.	APP II c.e.f.
	3rd		Short were noisal amount during the period under review.	
			Training was carried out in accordance with APP III	APP III c.e.f.
	4th		4 O.Rs went out to Corps Concentration Camp.	
			A few showers, sun shone at intervals.	
			Training was carried out in accordance with APP IV.	APP IV c.e.f.
	5th		Dull, there was several showers of rain. Very strong wind.	
			Church Parades took place during the morning. The C.O. held a conference at B.H.Q. at 12.00	
			Coy Cmds & Seconds in command of Coys attended. The question of handing in motor stores to Fn QM was discussed.	c.e.f.
	6th		Dull, Strong wind, sun shone during afternoon	
			Training was carried out in accordance with APP V	APP V c.e.f.
	7th		Sun, c.e.f.	
			Training was carried out. A draft of 55 O.R. (Reinforcements) joined from M & C Base	
			Depot. A draft of 11 Snrs joined from A.H.T.D.	c.e.f.
	8th		Sun, sun shone all day	
			Training was carried out. 12 O.Rs proceeded to Corps Concentration camp to be dematerialised	c.e.f.

(A7592) Wt. W12889/M1293. 75,000. 7/17. D. D. & L., Ltd. Forms/C.2118/14

Army Form C. 2118.

WAR DIARY
or
INTELLIGENCE SUMMARY.
(Erase heading not required.)

Instructions regarding War Diaries and Intelligence Summaries are contained in F. S. Regs., Part II. and the Staff Manual respectively. Title pages will be prepared in manuscript.

Place	Date	Hour	Summary of Events and Information	Remarks and references to Appendices
VELAINE	9th		Rain fell during morning, fine & sunny afternoon.	ccf
	10th		Training was carried out. 11 O.Rs proceeded to Con. Camp to be demobilized	ccf
			Fine, sun shone all day, cold	
	11th		Training was carried out. All men bathed during the day. 12 O.Rs proceeded to Con Camp to be demobilized	ccf
			Dull, rain fell during the day, cold.	
			Training was carried out.	ccf
	12th		Fine, dull, cold, rain fell during the night	
			Church Parade took place during the morning	ccf
	13th		Fine, dull, windy.	
			Training was carried out in accordance with APP VII	APP VII
			The Divisional Commander called during the morning	ccf
	14th		Fine, windy, dull. Rain fell during night	
			Training was carried out. 6 O.R. were despatched to Corps Con. Camp for demobilization.	ccf
	15th		Rainy, windy	
			Training was carried out. 7 O.R. were despatched to Corps Con camp for demobilization	ccf
			Fine, sun shone all day.	
	16th		Training was carried out. 6 O.R. were despatched to Corps Con camp for demobilization	ccf
			Showery, dull.	
	17th		Training was carried out.	ccf
			Dull, several showers of rain.	
	18th		Training was carried out	ccf

Army Form C. 2118.

WAR DIARY
or
INTELLIGENCE SUMMARY.
(Erase heading not required.)

Instructions regarding War Diaries and Intelligence Summaries are contained in F. S. Regs., Part II. and the Staff Manual respectively. Title pages will be prepared in manuscript.

Place	Date	Hour	Summary of Events and Information	Remarks and references to Appendices
VELAINE	19th		Dull but fine, misty & frosty at night. Church Parade took place during the morning. 11 OR were despatched for Demobilization.	ccf
	20th		Frosty, sun shone all day. Training was carried out in accordance with APP VII.	APP VII
			The Divisional Commander presented medal ribbons at 12.00 hrs. Col Appleton DSO gave a lecture to the battalion during the afternoon on "Demobilization and Reconstruction". 17 OR were despatched to Corps Dem Camp for demobilization.	ccf
	21st		Frosty, cold, sun shone all day. 17 OR were carried out.	ccf
	22nd		Training was carried out. 17 OR were despatched to Corps Con Camp for demobilization	ccf
	23rd		Frosty, cold, sun shone all day. 15 OR were despatched to Corps Con Camp for demobilization	ccf
	24th		Frosty, very cold, sunny. Training was carried out.	ccf
	25th		Frosty & very cold, sun shone all day. Training was carried out. All Coys routine	ccf
	26th		Very cold & frosty, sun shone. Training was carried out. 1 Officer & 14 OR were despatched for demobilization	ccf
	27th		Very cold, snow fell intermittently throughout the day, dull. Church Parade took place during the morning. 13 OR were despatched for demobilization	ccf
	28th		Very cold, dull. Training was carried out. 12 OR were despatched for demobilization	ccf

Army Form C. 2118.

WAR DIARY
or
INTELLIGENCE SUMMARY.
(Erase heading not required.)

Instructions regarding War Diaries and Intelligence Summaries are contained in F. S. Regs., Part II. and the Staff Manual respectively. Title pages will be prepared in manuscript.

Place	Date	Hour	Summary of Events and Information	Remarks and references to Appendices
VILAINE	28th	(cont)	Training was carried out. 1/2 O.R. were despatched to Corps Con camp for demobilization	ref
	29th		Cold, snow fell	ref
			Training was carried out. 3 O.R. were despatched to Corps Con camp for demobilization	
	30th		Cold, snow fell	ref
			Training was carried out.	
	31st		Cold, snow fell	ref
			Training was carried out	

Stoker Major
Cmg. 1/2nd Bn H.G.C.

APP I

TRAINING PROGRAMME, 1st January, 1919.

A. Coy.   **B. Coy.**

0745 - 0815 Brisk March
0930   Coy. Parade.   0745 - 0815 Brisk March
1000 - 1045 P.T.   0930   Coy. Parade.
1100 - 1145 Squad Drill   1000 - 1045 P.T.
1145 - 1230 Kit Inspection   1100 - 1145 Squad and Arm Drill
                                                 1145 - 1230 Care and Cleaning

C. Coy.   **D. Coy.**

0745 - 0815 Brisk March   0745 - 0815 Brisk March
0930   Coy. Parade   0930   Coy. Parade
1000 - 1045 P.T.   1000 - 1045 P.T.
1100 - 1145 Care & Cleaning   1100 - 1145 Care and Cleaning
1145 - 1230 Map Reading   1145 - 1230 Lecture
                                                             "History of M.G.C."

AFTERNOON :   All Coys.   RECREATIONAL TRAINING

All work is being done in the vicinity of billets.

Capt & Adj
42nd Bn M.G.C.

APP. II

2nd. Battalion H.G.C.

TRAINING PROGRAMME FOR THURSDAY 2nd. JANUARY 1919.

'A' Coy.	'B' Coy.	'C' Coy.	'D' Coy.
0745 - 0815	All Companies	Brisk March	
0830	- do -	Company Parade.	
1000 - 1045	- do -	P.T.	
1100 - 1145	1100 - 1200	1100 - 1200	1100 - 1115.
Squad and Arms Drill.	Squad and Arms Drill	Squad Drill	Musketry
1145 - 1230	1200 - 1300		1115 - 1230
Instruction and Recognition.	Care and Cleaning.		Musketry, Care & Cleaning.

A F T E R N O O N   Recreational Training.

All the above training will take place in the vicinity of Madlets.
E.P.
1.1.19.

CC Rose Capt. & Adjt.
2nd. Battalion H.G.C.

App III

TRAINING PROGRAMME for 3/1/19.
42nd. Battalion, M.G.C.

```
0745 - 0815   All Companies - Brisk March
0930             "       "     Company Parade
1000 - 1045      "       "     P.T.
```

'A' Coy.	'B' Coy.	'C' Coy.	'D' Coy.
1100 - 1200	1100 - 1130	1100	1100 - 1200
Care & Cleaning	Squad Drill	Lecture by C.O.	Use of Ground & Cover
1200 - 1230	1200 -	1200 - 1230	1200 - 1230
Squad Drill	Lecture by C.O.	Map Reading	Care & Cleaning

All work will take place in the vicinity of billets.

AFTERNOON - Recreational Training.

2/1/19.

Biddulph Lt. for
Capt. & Adjt.
for/O.C. 42nd. Battalion, M.G.C.

APP IV

42nd BATTALION, MACHINE GUN CORPS.
TRAINING PROGRAMME FOR SATURDAY, JANUARY 4th 1919.

'A' Company.   'B' Company.   'C' Company.   'D' Company.

0745 - 0815.   All Companies.   Brisk March.

0930.   "   "   Company Parade.

1000 - 1045.   "   "   P.T.

'A' Company	'B' Company	'C' Company	'D' Company
1100 - 1130. Lecture by C.O.	1100 - 1130. Squad Drill.	1100 - 1130. Interior Economy.	1100 - 1130. Interior Economy.
1140 - 1210. Squad & Arms Drill.	1130 - 1230. Kit Inspection. Cleaning Billets.		1130 - 1200. Lecture by C.O.
1210 - 1230. Preparing Guns for Firing.			1200 - 1230. Interior Economy.

All work will take place in the vicinity of billets.

AFTERNOON   -   RECREATIONAL TRAINING.

T.P.
3.1.19.

                   Capt. for O.C.,
                   42nd. Battalion, M.G.C.

APP V

42nd BATTALION, MACHINE GUN CORPS.
TRAINING PROGRAMME FOR WEEK ENDING JANUARY 11th. 1919.

---oOo---

MILITARY TRAINING.

        Individual training.
        Musketry - Squad Drill - Handling of Arms -
        Saluting etc.
        M.G. Competitions on the Range.
        Physical Training.
        Lectures.
        Recreational Training every afternoon.

Educational Training.

        Not yet commenced.

        All training will take place in vicinity of
VELAINE.

T.P.
5.1.19.
           CC Rose   Capt. for O.C.,
                 42nd. Battalion, M.G.C.

APP VI

42nd BATTALION, MACHINE GUN CORPS.
TRAINING PROGRAMME FOR WEEK ENDING JANUARY 18th. 1919.
---oOo---

<u>MILITARY TRAINING.</u>
        Individual Training.
        Musketry.
        Steady Drill.
        Saluting.
        Physical Training.
        Competitions.
        Recreational Training.

<u>EDUCATIONAL TRAINING.</u>
        Artificer.
        Farriery.
        Carpentry.
        Horsemanship (including riding).
%   Lectures.
        Boot Repairing.
        Tailoring.

% At the moment we are very short of suitable Officer Instructors.

All training will take place in vicinity of VELAINE.

T.P.
12.1.19.

                        CCRose
                        Capt for Major,
               Cmdg. 42nd. Battalion, M.G.C.

APP VII

42nd. BATTALION, MACHINE GUN CORPS,
TRAINING PROGRAMME FOR WEEK ENDING JANUARY 25th. 1919.

---oOo---

MILITARY TRAINING.
    Individual Training.
    Presentation of Medals.
    Steady Drill.
    Saluting.
    Short Lectures.
    Recreational Training.

EDUCATIONAL TRAINING.
    Attachment to Workshops.
    Horsemanship.
    French.
    Arithmetic.
    Reading and Writing.
    English Literature.
    Shorthand.
    Lectures.

All Training will take place in the vicinity of VELAINE.

T.P.
19.1.19.

Capt.,
for O.C. 42nd. Battalion M.G. Corps.

APP VIII

42ND. BATTALION, MACHINE GUN CORPS.
TRAINING PROGRAMME FOR WEEK ENDING FEBRUARY 1st. 1919.

MILITARY TRAINING.

    Individual training.
    Steady Drill.
    Saluting.
    P.T.
    Short Lectures.
    Recreational Training.

EDUCATIONAL TRAINING.

    Attachment to Workshops.
    Horsemastership.
    French.
    Arithmetic.
    Reading & Writing.
    English Literature.
    Shorthand.
    Lectures on Poultry Farming.
    Spanish.

T.P.
25.1.19.

ccRose
Capt. for O.C.,
42nd. Battalion, M.G.C.

Vol 12

Confidential
(original)

WAR DIARY

OF

42nd Battalion M.G.C.

From 1.2.19   To 28.2.19

Volume II

Army Form C. 2118.

WAR DIARY
or
INTELLIGENCE SUMMARY.
(Erase heading not required.)

Instructions regarding War Diaries and Intelligence Summaries are contained in F. S. Regs., Part II. and the Staff Manual respectively. Title pages will be prepared in manuscript.

Place	Date	Hour	Summary of Events and Information	Remarks and references to Appendices
VELAINE	1st		Frosty, very cold. Training was carried out in accordance with APPI. 1 Officer and 2 ORs left unit for demobilization	See APPI
	2nd		Dull & cold. 15 ORs were despatched to Corps Concentration Camp for demobilization. Church parade took place during the morning	See
	3rd		Dull & cold. Training was carried out. 14 ORs left unit for demobilization	See APPI
	4th		Cold, snow fell during afternoon. Training was carried out in accordance with APPI	See APPI
	5th		Cold, snow fell during afternoon. Training was carried out	See APPI
	6th		Cold, sun shone at intervals. Training was carried out. 2 Officers and 81 ORs were despatched to Corps Concentration Camp for demobilization	See APPI
	7th		Sun shone at intervals. Training was carried out. 1 Officer & 12 ORs left unit for demobilization	See APPI
	8th		Training as usual, football during the afternoon. 11 ORs left unit for demobilization, weather fine & frosty. Sun shining all day.	See APPI
	9th		Church Parade 10th Hour on the morning, weather frosty & frosty. Sun shining all day.	See

Army Form C. 2118.

WAR DIARY
or
INTELLIGENCE SUMMARY.
(Erase heading not required.)

Instructions regarding War Diaries and Intelligence Summaries are contained in F. S. Regs., Part II. and the Staff Manual respectively. Title pages will be prepared in manuscript.

Place	Date	Hour	Summary of Events and Information	Remarks and references to Appendices
VELAINE	10th		Fine & frosty, sun shone all day. Training as usual.	98
	11th		Sun shone all day. Training as usual.	98
	12th		Sun shone during morning, dull in afternoon. Training carried out. 6 O.R.'s left unit for demobilization.	98
	13th		Dull & cold, rain fell during afternoon. Training carried out.	98
	14th		6 O.R.'s left unit for demobilization. Rain fell during day. Training as usual.	98
	15th		2 officers & 30 O.R.'s left unit for demobilization. Dull, sun shone at intervals. Training as usual. 5 O.R.'s left unit for demobilization.	98
	16th		Dull & cold, rain fell during afternoon. Stood parades took place during morning. 6 O.R.'s left unit for demobilization.	98
	17th		Dull, rain fell during day. Training as usual.	98

WAR DIARY
or
INTELLIGENCE SUMMARY.
(Erase heading not required.)

Army Form C. 2118.

Instructions regarding War Diaries and Intelligence Summaries are contained in F. S. Regs. Part II. and the Staff Manual respectively. Title pages will be prepared in manuscript.

Place	Date	Hour	Summary of Events and Information	Remarks and references to Appendices
VELAINE	18th		Dull, rain fell during day. Training as usual	AB
	19th		6 ORs left unit for demobilization. Games were played during afternoon	AB
	20th		Dull, sun shone at intervals. Training as usual. 2 ORs left unit for demobilization. Recreational Training during afternoon	AB
	21st		Cloudy, sun shone at intervals. Training as usual. 3 ORs left unit for demobilization. Recreational training during afternoon	AB
	22nd		Bright, sun shone at intervals, strong wind. 1 OR left unit for demobilization. Recreational training during afternoon	AB
	23rd		Bright, sun shone at intervals. 6 ORs left unit for demobilization. Recreational training during afternoon	AB
	24th		Dull, rain fell during the day. Church Parade took place during the morning. Recreational training during afternoon	AB
	25th		Dull, sun shone at intervals. Recreational training during afternoon	AB
	26th		Dull, rain fell during day. Recreational training during afternoon	AB

Army Form C. 2118.

WAR DIARY
or
INTELLIGENCE SUMMARY.
(Erase heading not required.)

Instructions regarding War Diaries and Intelligence Summaries are contained in F. S. Regs., Part II. and the Staff Manual respectively. Title pages will be prepared in manuscript.

Place	Date	Hour	Summary of Events and Information	Remarks and references to Appendices
VELAINE	26th		Bright, sun shone during day. 2 Q.M. stores, lignite depots & spare parts were handed into dump at Shatlins. Resumed training during afternoon.	98
	27th		Dull, rain fell during day. 2 Q.M. stores, pack saddles & hit racks were handed into dump at Shatlins. Resumed training during afternoon.	98
	28th		Bright, sun shone during day. Limbers & stores were handed into dump at Shatlins. Resumed training during afternoon.	98

B.R. Tucker
Lt Col
Commanding 42nd Batt. M.G.C.

APP I

42ND. BATTALION, MACHINE GUN CORPS.
TRAINING PROGRAMME FOR WEEK ENDING FEBRUARY 8th, 1919.
———oOo———

MILITARY TRAINING.
        Individual training.
        Steady Drill.
        Recreational Training.

EDUCATIONAL TRAINING.
        Horsemastership.
        French.
        Arithmetic.
        Reading & Writing.
        Spanish.
        Shorthand.

T.P.
2.2.19.

                                              CC Rose
                                                  Capt. for O.C.,
                                      42nd. Battalion, M.G.C.

42

Vol 13

42nd Battalion M.G.C.

War Diary.

for

March 1919.

42ND BATTALION.
MACHINE GUN
CORPS.
No. M.G./852
Date

Army Form C. 2118.

WAR DIARY
or
INTELLIGENCE SUMMARY.
(Erase heading not required.)

Instructions regarding War Diaries and Intelligence Summaries are contained in F. S. Regs., Part II. and the Staff Manual respectively. Title pages will be prepared in manuscript.

Place	Date	Hour	Summary of Events and Information	Remarks and references to Appendices
VELAINE	1st		Bright, sun shone during day. Continued to hand in stores to dump at Charleroi. Recreational training during afternoon	7x8
	2nd		Dull, rain fell at intervals during day. Stores were handed into dump at Charleroi. 4 y. animals were despatched for England. Recreational training during afternoon	7x8
	3rd		Dull, rain shower at intervals. Recreational training during afternoon	7x8
	4th		Dull, rain fell during day. 23 horses & 30 mules were despatched to Auxiliary Remount stat[io]n. Recreational training during afternoon	7x8
	5th		Dull during morning, rain shower during afternoon. Recreational training during afternoon	7x8
	6th		Dull, strong wind, rain fell during day. 12 y[eomanry]/Yeo 7.10 PM left unit for Demobilisation. 18 O.R. Yeomen[?] bayonet[?] for H[ot]land Army. 31 animals were despatched for H[eavy] Bat[tery] Carleon[?] stat[ion]	7x8
	7th		Dull, rain fell during day. Stores were handed into dump at Charleroi	7x8
	8th		Dull & cold, rain fell at intervals. Stores were handed into dump at Charleroi. Recreational training during afternoon	7x8

Army Form C. 2118.

WAR DIARY
or
INTELLIGENCE SUMMARY.
(Erase heading not required.)

Instructions regarding War Diaries and Intelligence Summaries are contained in F. S. Regs. Part II. and the Staff Manual respectively. Title pages will be prepared in manuscript.

Place	Date	Hour	Summary of Events and Information	Remarks and references to Appendices
VELAINE	9th		Bright, sun shone during day. Lt Col W.K. Title D.S.O. M.C. commanding 42nd Batt. M.G.C. left unit for demobilization. Stores were handed into dump at Shaleur.	JRB
MONTIGNY	10th		Church parade took place during morning. Recreational training during afternoon.	JRB
	11th		Dull & cold. Move of Battalion from Velaine to Montigny was completed.	JRB
	12th		Bright, mild wind, sun shone during afternoon. Stores were handed into dump at Battalion.	JRB
	13th		Cloudy, sun shone at intervals. Orders were received that Battalion was to be reorganised and proceed to the Rhine.	JRB
	14th		Cold & cloudy. E.O.R.'s + 10 H.D. horses joined unit from R.E's.	JRB
	15th		Dull & cold. Stores were drawn from dump at Shaleur.	JRB
	16th		Dull, sun shone at intervals during day. 2 officers + 130 O.R's left unit for demobilization.	JRB
VELAINE	17th		Bright, sun shone during day. Church parade took place during morning. Lt Col C.C. Hannett D.S.O. M.C. proceeded out to take over command. Dull, rain fell inland during day. Battalion moved from Montigny to Velaine. 10 O.R's left unit for demobilization.	JRB

WAR DIARY
or
INTELLIGENCE SUMMARY.

(Erase heading not required.)

Army Form C. 2118.

Instructions regarding War Diaries and Intelligence Summaries are contained in F. S. Regs., Part II. and the Staff Manual respectively. Title pages will be prepared in manuscript.

March 19

Place	Date	Hour	Summary of Events and Information	Remarks and references to Appendices
VELAINE	18th		Dull & showery. Stores were drawn from dump at Charleroi	App 8
	19th		Dull sun at moment intervals during day. "A.O.R." left unit for demobilization	App 8
	20th		Dull & showery. Stores & clothing were drawn from dump at Charleroi	App 8
	21st		Cloudy, sun shone at intervals during day. Recreational training during afternoon	App 3
	22nd		Dull & wet. Recreational training during afternoon	App 8
	23rd		Bright, sun shone during day. Recreational training during afternoon	App 8
	24th		Dull & cold, snow fell during morning. Recreational training during afternoon	App 8
	25th		Dull & wet. Recreational training during afternoon	App 8
	26th		Dull & cold. Recreational training during afternoon	App 3

Army Form C. 2118.

WAR DIARY
or
INTELLIGENCE SUMMARY.
(Erase heading not required.)

Instructions regarding War Diaries and Intelligence Summaries are contained in F. S. Regs., Part II. and the Staff Manual respectively. Title pages will be prepared in manuscript.

Place	Date	Hour	Summary of Events and Information	Remarks and references to Appendices
VELAINE	27th		Rest & cleaning.	#3
	28th		B.O.R.s left ward for demobilization. 18th only joined the unit from 16th, 26th & 31st Battalion. Rest & wet snow fell during day.	#3
	29th		Rest & cold, snow fell during day. 97 O.R.s joined unit from 18th Battalion.	#8
	30th		Showery snow storm at intervals. Church parade (RC) held during the morning.	#3
	31st		Bath & Rest, troops warned of possibility of epidemic. Parade in the morning & practice in gas appliances.	#8

D.A.A.G.,
VI CORPS.
No. A.15.614
Date 7/6/19

HQ VI Corps.

Herewith War Diary for month of May 1919

B J Cowan Capt
f Maj Cmdg
42nd Battn
M G C.

6/6/19

42ND BATTALION,
MACHINE GUN
CORPS.
No. MG/655.
Date

Confidential.

War Diary.

42nd. Bn. M.G. Corps.

May 1st. 1919.
to
May 31st. 1919.

B. Brown. CAPT. & ADJT.
42nd BN. MACHINE GUN CORPS.

42nd BATTALION.
MACHINE GUN
CORPS.
Date June 6. 1919

WAR DIARY
or
INTELLIGENCE SUMMARY.
(Erase heading not required.)

Army Form C. 2118.

Place	Date	Hour	Summary of Events and Information	Remarks and references to Appendices
MUNGERSDORF	May 1	dull	Parade. Batt. Training	Afternoon recreational training	B.9c
	2	dull	— do —	— do —	B.9c
	3	dull	— do —	— do —	B.9c
	4	fine	Sunday. Church Parade	1 Officer & N.C.O.'s to demolition	B.9c
	5		Parade. Batt Training	Afternoon recreational training	B.9c
	6		Parade	6 Officers & N.C.O.'s to dem Pltn	B.9c
	7		— do —	Afternoon recreational training	B.9c
	8		— do —	— do —	B.9c
	9		Parade	dem. off. to demolition	B.9c
	10		Parade	— do —	B.9c
	11	fully Sunday	Church Parade	— do —	B.9c
	12	fine	Parade. Batt Training	Afternoon recreational training	B.9c
	13	fine	Parade	50 O.R. & 6 Offrs Tpt to Rhine	B.9c
	14	rain	Parade	—	B.9c
	15	—	Parade	Afternoon recreational in armoury	B.9c
	16	—	Parade	— do —	B.9c
	17	—	Parade	—	B.9c
	18		Parade Church Parade	Calendar day 10th Batt. of Battalion	B.9c
			Sunday Church Parades	N Offrs sent to demobilization	B.9c
	19		Pdes. Batt. Training	Afternoon recreational training	B.9c

WAR DIARY
or
INTELLIGENCE SUMMARY.
(Erase heading not required.)

Army Form C. 2118.

Instructions regarding War Diaries and Intelligence Summaries are contained in F.S. Regs., Part II. and the Staff Manual respectively. Title pages will be prepared in manuscript.

Place	Date	Hour	Summary of Events and Information	Remarks and references to Appendices
Bunjaradag	May 20	9am	Parade. Batt. Training 5 ORs. 16 Offr. Took up Plng. Offrs. educational training	8/c
	21	—	Parade. Batt. training	8/c
	22	—	Rath Training. 200 Anionk expended	8/c
	23	—	Parade. Batt Training	8/c
	24	—	Parade. Batt. Training	8/c
	25	—	Sunday. Church Parade	8/c
	26	—	346 ORs evacuated 6 2nd Batts. 296 + 15 Officers evacuated 641st Batt. 29 animal evacuated	8/c
	27	—	Cleaning rebythin of stores.	8/c
	28	—	10 Officer evacuated 2nd Batt. Batt. prctg. stores	8/c
	29	—	Draft of 76 ORs arrived from 10th Batt.	8/c
	30	—	Draft evacuated 30 6 41st Batt + 3 Pts. 2nd Batt. 4 Offrs. arr. Kennedyala Ein	8/c
	31	—	Parades. Batt Training	8/c

Commandant,
    VI Corps Troops.

> 42ND BATTALION, MACHINE GUN CORPS.
> No. MG/788/10

        Herewith War Diary for this Battalion for the Month of June.1919.

July.3rd.1919.   J.Browe Lt/a Capt.,
                            for.O.C. 42nd. Bn. Machine Gun Corps.

SECRET.

ORIGINAL.

WAR DIARY.

42ND BATTALION.

MACHINE GUN CORPS.

JUNE 1919.

Army Form C. 2118.

WAR DIARY
or
INTELLIGENCE SUMMARY.
(Erase heading not required.)

Instructions regarding War Diaries and Intelligence Summaries are contained in F.S. Regs., Part II. and the Staff Manual respectively. Title pages will be prepared in manuscript.

Place	Date	Hour	Summary of Events and Information	Remarks and references to Appendices
Mingoudorf	June 1919 1	full	Sunday Church Parade	BfC
	2	null	Batt returned to strength of Cadre	BfC
	3	full cast	Packing of Equipment	BfC
	4	-do-	-do-	BfC
	5	-do-	-do-	BfC
	6	-do-	-do-	
	7	-do-	-do- 4 Officers sent to Depot Batt at	
	8	2.30	-do- 6.6. Batt (of 51 Bedford No)	
	9		Officers transferred	
	10		⎫	
	11		⎪	
	12		⎪	
	13		⎬ Packing +	BfC
	14		⎪ Landing in of	
	15		⎪ Stores	
	16		⎭	
	17			
	18			
	19			
	20			
	21			
	22			
	23			
	24			

Army Form C. 2118.

WAR DIARY
or
INTELLIGENCE SUMMARY.
(Erase heading not required.)

Instructions regarding War Diaries and Intelligence Summaries are contained in F. S. Regs., Part II. and the Staff Manual respectively. Title pages will be prepared in manuscript.

Place	Date	Hour	Summary of Events and Information	Remarks and references to Appendices
Mhungerd	June 25		Packing and loading	
	26		w/ of Store	
	27			
	28			
	29			
	30			

www.ingramcontent.com/pod-product-compliance
Lightning Source LLC
Chambersburg PA
CBHW081353160426
43192CB00013B/2401